The Italian Chronicles of a Rogue Tourist

Volume I

Discovering Calitri

Paul D. Monico

First Edition

ISBN 9780979623394

Printed by Riverside Press, Cummington MA 01026

Acknowledgements

In compiling these tales, I wish to thank the people of Italy and especially my wonderful Calitri friends and neighbors. Without them, this book would not have been possible.

I must also thank the persistent voices of my many readers, who over the years suggested and eventually convinced me to compile my memories and reflections into book form.

I am also grateful for the steadfast help, the many excellent suggestions, and the invaluable assistance with publishing provided from my editor, Bailly Morse. Her know-how made the journey from red scrawled edits to completed book a pleasant experience, far from rocky shoals.

Most of all, I am forever grateful to my wife, constant travel companion and toughest critic, Mary Ellen, alias Maria Elena. There are few women like her willing to climb pyramids, travel through underground channels knee deep in rushing water and in general, put up with the antics of a Rogue Tourist.

Discovering Calitri

Contents

(The Years 2006 - 2008)

1. Paolo and Maria Elena relaxing, Lake Como

"These are the Experiences of an American Couple, Who in a 2006 Leap of Faith Purchased Casa della Feritoia, Now Their Retreat in Southern Italy. Enjoy their Personal Collection of Travel Memories and Italian Adventures including long Tales, Photo Albums and Video Clips. Welcome to Their Impressions of Bella Italia and all Things Italian, Wherever They May be Found."

Introduction

The first words of a story are important. They serve as that first spoonful of sustenance that nourishes the reader and hopefully coaxes them into believing, if not saying aloud, "This was a worthwhile read, a good story." Elizabeth Taylor once said, *"Everyone should have a chance at a breathtaking piece of folly at least once in their life."*

Thus far, our folly has been Calitri, positioned on a bluff halfway between Naples on the left coast of Italy and Bari on the right. On the day of our arrival in Calitri, a town official approached us in the *Piazza della Repubblica*. Curious, in his best English he asked, "Why you come here?"

Caught off-guard, all I managed to say in reply was that while visitors flock to the art cities of Rome, Florence, and Venice, what I like to call *The Big Three*, this town was the other side of Italy and to me represented the real face of Italy. *The Big Three* are no more representative of Italy than Los Angeles, Las Vegas or New York City mirror average life in America. Our fascination with Calitri, our Calitri folly, quickly morphed into an enduring love of Italy.

The tales that fill this book originated from that first visit as monthly inputs to an online blog, which began with the words in italics above. Far from the norm of most blogs, however, where paragraph size comments and maybe a photo or two satisfied the appetite of social media, I began to go farther.

My wife and travel companion, Mary Ellen (alias Maria Elena) has often accused me of never using a word I'd willingly redact. Apparently, I liked them all. What the heck, each month I felt I had a story worth relating that by the end of my telling, looked, due to its length, more and more like the chapter of a book.

Whether they should be called a compilation of travel essays, or better yet, a travelogue, I still wondered why I was motivated to write accounts of our Italian travels each month. There are multiple motives, though none in itself offers a full explanation. One reason is simply that I enjoy writing. In some way, it was also about immortality, for I wanted to leave some trace of myself to posterity. Recently while reading a book about Caesar, the author mentioned the entire lack of writing by the common people of Rome. They never got to recount their side of the Empire's story. Just maybe in a thousand years, a billion bytes by me (alias Paolo) might still be surging through the ether, as fresh as spring flowers, recounting our days in Calitri. Maybe that's a little piece of why.

Another motive may bear witness to a selfish side of me, for I began to write of our Italian adventures for myself. When I began, I had no intention of writing a book. We do with memories what we wish, and I was simply capturing memories of Italy, especially those involving Calitri, one recollection at a time. Over our many trips, we had brought back mental pieces of Italy, like people return from vacations with souvenirs. But how do you capture memories to bring home? Photos help but even those become jumbled, misplaced, or if they survive, difficult to later fix in space and time. Memories can't be unwrapped and set on a shelf like some tchotchke, to dust occasionally as you smile at the thought or emotion each evokes. Over time our memories no longer remain. A sort of seen it, done it, can't seem to remember any of it mood sets in. Remembrances, the people we met, and the places we'd visited undoubtedly fade to a weedy patch of vague memories, to be easily confused with other recollections, until thoughts of Italy would amount to nothing more specific than a smile and warm feeling when someone mentioned the place or poured me a glass of *vino*. Fact is, when a story is written, it is not easily forgotten. So with a touch of hedonism, I began to write.

There was one other motive that eventually took hold. I wanted a greater audience to feel as we had. I wanted others to share in the Italian experience and that sense of Calitri and its people. I began talking to my unseen readers. With any luck, the armchair traveler would be motivated to venture off, first to a travel agent and then to that out-of-the-ordinary place, so beautiful that they had to christen it "*Bella*."

Finally, like one of the electron characters in the movie *Tron*, my stories to this point lived in my computer on a sliver of silicon overseen by some *Intel* processor. They came to life at the click of a mouse and just as easily could be cubbyholed back into the void of the unconscious cyber-world of nothingness.

I felt they deserved better. I felt they were worthy of their own life, a full-time presence.

The rest came after I'd been faithfully writing tales, one a month, for over eight years. They include tales of how we came to discover Italy, our decision to establish roots in bucolic Calitri, our Italian travels and much, much more of our Italian evolution, ultimately leading to Italian citizenship. These stories began to emerge from the moment we were asked, "Why you come here?" Encouraging readers suggested I gather my monthlies and compose them into a narrative of travel memories and impressions. Reviewing their many topics and oftentimes re-experiencing the emotion they imparted about Italy, I decided to chance publishing this collection of memoirs, each volume containing a year or more compilation of essays. Hopefully, you will enjoy my little electrons, my screed now in book-form, enough to call it "a good read."

Lost in small town Italy and cut from the whole cloth of our experiences, welcome to blog the book, *The Italian Chronicles of a Rogue Tourist: Vol I - Discovering Calitri*, our Italian world. *Divertiti* (Enjoy)!

From That Rogue Tourist
Paolo

Part I

Experiencing Calitri

2. Paolo tries on an Ape for size

The word *borgo* is Italian for village. The small town of Calitri is unique in that its roots lie in a true medieval village. With its cobbled streets once restricted to the passage of pedestrians on foot, and horses and mules of old, today most still remain too narrow for automobiles to negotiate. Our home away, *Casa della Feritoia* (House of the Arrow Slit), lies among these narrow lanes in the heart of Calitri's Borgo.

Of uncertain origin, its first settlers are lost in time. Most likely they chose to colonize the area for its convenience as a trade route, connecting the Tyrrhenian Sea to the west and the Adriatic coast, almost equidistant to the east. To an extent, Calitri is still lost in time, remaining a place the pages of international guide books haven't yet discovered.

In these opening excerpts of a longer story, I describe how we settled on Calitri as our Italian *pied à terre* foothold and describe some of the people we have met, and the places we've visited, from homes and restaurants to dark caverns in the earth beneath Calitri, now home to bats and ageing cheeses. All along this journey of discovery, I share the infectious enthusiasm and emotion we experienced.

Today, Calitri is experiencing an influx of European and American ex-patriots eager to immerse themselves in the Italian dream, whether it be in the form of its particular Mediterranean diet, its deliberate slower pace from the hectic seemingly distant world outside, or the warm friendliness of its inhabitants.

3. Hillside of Antico Borgo, Calitri

1

What's in a Name?

When writing these Italian tales as a blog, I utilized *casacalitri* as my handle. This seemed fitting, as *casa* means house, and Calitri is the place that we call our home away from home. If you are like a majority of folks, you might be asking, well, where on the Italian boot is Calitri? Calitri is situated in the Campania region of southern Italy, with Naples as its capital. There are about 6000 inhabitants in Calitri and we can now claim to be a couple of them, that is, on those occasions when we can get over there. First, a little ancient history. The test will follow later:

In the first century AD, in a 37 book masterpiece, Historia Naturalis, considered the pinnacle of ancient encyclopedias, the author, Roman Pliny the Elder (23AD - 79AD) listed the Aletrini together with all the subjects of the Roman Empire in Book III. In this extensive work, the community is referred to as Aletrium. Aletrium was an ancient, important commercial center at the time of the Roman Empire. Much later the name was changed into Caletrum and finally Calitri. During the 11th century it was ruled by the Count of Conza, then for 3 centuries it was under the Gesualdo family. In 1636, Francesco Mirelli bought the fiefdom. Unfortunately on Sept 8, 1694, a ruinous earthquake destroyed a great part of Calitri, including the old castle, killing over 300 people. Nowadays it is renowned for its artistic ceramics.[1]

We doubt a future Pliny will be writing about us, but we like it there. Its character, people, and atmosphere are inviting for anyone looking to get off the *Big Three* circuit (Roma, Firenze and Venezia) and find their personal corner of Italy, little changed from the past. The medieval *borgo* that runs down one side of the mountain from which Calitri commands the countryside seems like a historic time-capsule. The views to the east reveal the beginnings of Basilicata, which puts us just about smack dab in the center of the peninsula called Italy and on the far right side of that Italian region known as Campania. It's one of those places where the streets are so narrow in places that cars can't navigate them and stairways and alleys serve to connect the streets (one above the other), which run parallel to each other and sit terrace-like as they spill down the mountainside.

The photo above is a snapshot of *Antico Borgo* Calitri (its more modern counterpart is on the other side of the mountain). Our little place is in there but more about that on another day.

December, 2006

---

1   For a helpful guide to regions in Italy, visit the Italy World Club website, <http://www.italyworldclub.com/campania/avelli-no/calitri.htm>

2

What's in a Face?

My wife and partner in this adventure, Maria Elena, enjoys the pictures I snap of streaming strings of laundry suspended from small balconies or stretching across some alleyway that we sometimes glimpse in our ramblings through Italy. These fluttering pendants of home-life must have something to do with a shared common bond or maybe some symbol of family and nurturing, I'm not sure. She also enjoys the pictures I take of Italians we meet and even of those we sometimes don't really meet in a formal sense: that fleeting passerby, for example.

4. Face of man on street, Taormina, Sicily

If I am inclined to take a picture, I'll first ask permission. To this point, by the way, my only refusal was from a nun in

Taormina! Oh well, her loss.

There is something magical about a face. Faces tell us things. Some contend that a face is a reflection of one's inner soul, mirroring inner emotions. Do our first impressions owe their formation to that smile, that frown, or that *Marlboro Man* rugged sort of look? No doubt we form judgments, for better or worse, leading to the assignment of personal traits based on someone's expression, their mystery, or their general appearance. Does it tell of the life lived (or not lived), a sadness, their spirit and gusto for life or possibly of some hardship? I feel there is a little of all that plus the mystique of the person — sort of like when we say "if only these walls could talk"— in a face. What does that face tell us? What's in a face?

Italy has many faces (*facce*). Here are but two of my faces, the *Facce d'Italia*. Enjoy.

December, 2006.

5. Face of market-day vendor, Calitri

3

A World is Flat Attitude

My hypothesis is that you have to be a special breed of person to run off and buy a place in far off Italy. Some might go so far as to say certifiably nuts. I wouldn't blame them. We were ourselves on and off, hot and cold for some time on the decision to actually jump in. It's like how I felt when I first jumped, or at least attempted to jump, off the high diving board as a kid. I wanted to so badly, but was apprehensive to actually take that final step. First time jitters, fears, even backing down the ladder to the protests of the other kids, sometimes won out. Buy a place in Italy?

Then we started thinking... Others have done this, why not us? Good investment? We love to travel and Italy

6. As we found it in 2006, Casa della Feritoia, Calitri

is our preferred destination, so why not get a home there to use in retirement? Thoughts like these ran through our heads. And then there was that more rational side of our brains that questioned how much we'd ever use a retreat in Italy, no matter how fabulous and romantic. Or the even more sobering thought, why tie ourselves down and have to always restrict our Italian adventures to medieval Calitri? I think it was my wife, Maria Elena, who first voiced that one. These, and many, many other micro-volts of thoughts, swirled in our heads. But jump in we did. It takes a sort of leap of faith, equivalent to actually stepping off that diving board, out into the unknown and unfamiliar.

The rest of the adventure, to this point, has been exciting and exhilarating and we haven't even hit the water yet! It has definitely been a life changing experience.

For the non-faint-of-heart and those endowed with a dash of impulsive adventurism, I can honestly say, "You can do it". It also helps that we live in an ever-increasing global community where people, money, products, and information move fluidly around the globe as never before, and where it is no longer unreasonable to think globally, commute globally, invest globally, and live globally.

The advent of the Internet also helped tremendously. It allows people to be empowered as never before. Honestly, without the Internet, none of this would be possible. Besides, hasn't Airbus built a new, 800-plus supersized passenger aircraft (A380), that dwarfs the B747? Who will fill these seats? It's Baby Boomers like us, on the cusp of retiring, who are beginning

7. Casa della Feritoia, 2007

to deploy worldwide to places like *Bella Italia.*

The name of our Italian foothold is *Casa della Feritoia,* translated as best I can as House of the Arrow Slit. Yes, as in narrow opening through which you could shoot arrows at attackers. There is a castle farther-up the hillside behind us, so once upon a time this circling band of homes, huddled together for protection, may have been part of a first line of defense. Better yet, this may have been how you determined whether to answer the door or not. Being a romantic, I want to believe everything about our root just grabbing hold in the boot of Italy.

Chiseled in stone over our entry door is the date 1875 and the initials "L.S.", but we're told it goes farther back than that. It is easy to believe, for each time we exit through this portal, like a talisman, our day blends into past as we enter the wonderment of Calitri.

By the way, we begin Italian classes at our local community college tonight.

January, 2007

**8. Front door, Casa della
Feritoia today, Borgo Calitri**

*"Two roads diverged in a wood, and I—
I took the one less traveled by,
And that has made all the difference."*

"The Road Not Taken" -
Robert Frost

4

There's a Place Called Home

After visiting Italy a number of times, I began to develop a desire to be there more and more. I don't know what this urge is called but there must be a name for it. I can't even recall why we ever decided to visit Italy in the first place. Yes, I was a second generation American Italian, yet I had an equal amount of French blood in me as well. There was no urge, however, to visit my Normandy ancestry. Was I becoming a wannabe Italian through some insidious process? Was it some yearning to return to my roots brought on by more virulent Italian genes?

As a child, I'd say the French influence was more dominant in my home. After all, my grandmother lived with us, and though she had years and years to learn English, she chose to speak only French. I'd describe her as a proud woman.

My father, on the other hand, really didn't know much Italian or vigorously promote his Italian heritage. Yes, there were the occasional Italian words thrown about, and yes, my mom learned to cook Italian food, mostly to keep dad happy. Overall, my greatest exposure to things Italian were those times I'd deliver the newspaper to the *Raucci and Vasile* Italian market in my hometown. The smells, the sawdust strewn across the floor, the open barrels of olives, the mysterious cans with flamboyant labels, and the sheets of *baccala* piled high, these were my true initiation. Imagine a place with meats and cheeses hanging from the ceiling! I guess I just loved the food and later the wines. My gradual conversion from half-blood was underway and the metamorphosis continued through a lifetime of reading, movies, the ever-growing positive reputation of Italy, and eventually my own travels in Italy. I was in love with my wife, my family, and now Italy.

Now, following many memorable and delightful experiences in Italy, we were at a fork in the road of life. Should we buy our own tiny piece of Italy and immerse ourselves in the culture, the language, and its people, or should we continue to wander the country continually visiting new places for there would always be new venues to explore. One road read 'come this way', the other, equally appealing, like a hawker in front of a restaurant, beckoned that we proceed down that avenue. Our quandary, which way to go? We were on and off, hot and cold for some time on whether to choose the purchase path, but as is now clear, this eventually was the course we chose.

We began this new phase in our lives and a new phase in our Italian adventure in June 2006, when we first visited Calitri. We were looking into the possibility of buying a place there, which we could eventually call home. Our intent was never to pick-up and move outright to Italy. Instead, our idea of an Italian home was a small affordable place we could use in retirement for a few months at a time, and even before that, as often as we could get there. Cost was also heavily weighted. For this reason we had gradually eliminated properties further north and moved steadily southward. A final criterion was location. We wanted to be situated in a town and not in some isolated spot out in the countryside. After all, that's where the culture and people were located. Additionally, it supplemented the physical security of our investment.

Located about midway between the coasts of the Italian peninsula, Calitri is approximately two hours from the Amalfi Coast and Pompeii to the west, and *Magna Graecia* and the Adriatic Sea to the east. Calitri sits on a plateau overlooking verdant rolling countryside just about on the border dividing Campania and Basilicata. Its undulating hills and valleys mark the ancient trails along which Hannibal and his army marched during the 2nd Punic War when setting off to attack ancient Rome 2,000 years ago. With its wine cellars, meandering medieval passageways, chiseled entranceways, marble engravings, and sun-kissed courtyards and rooftops, to this day it remains a snapshot of a bygone era, a place that inhabits the past.

The Calitri town council, working with some leading citizens and an Italy/UK based development firm, formed a relationship to redevelop this historic community, while protecting the town's environment and its cultural and artistic heritage. Calitri was heavily damaged by an earthquake in 1980 and has yet to fully recover. The *Borgo* area of town, a labyrinth of narrow streets and ancient dwellings hooked together in what I liken to a 'medieval condo', still needed major repairs.

By attracting property investors like ourselves, the town

council's vision anticipates an influx of capital sufficient to reinvigorate the *Borgo* hamlet by stimulating economic development, spanning the gamut from building repairs, jobs for local craftsmen, and new customers for everything from furniture and *vino* to increased cappuccino sales! The blueprint, now well underway, anticipates reconstructing/revitalizing up to 200 *Borgo* homes over a number of phases.

It was on 12 June 2006 that we became the 34th property investors in the project (one of a handful of Americans thus far) and began the purchase process. By the 16th of October with our new *codice fiscale* documents (think Italian tax card), we successfully closed on the property using a power of attorney and an agent as our stand-in. Within days, renovations, which thankfully were included in the purchase price, began. This activity finished just days ago (actually, we still need a back-ordered ceiling fan).

All in all, surprisingly, it was not too difficult an undertaking from beginning to end. We had heard horror stories of the disasters previous *immobiliare* (real estate) neophytes had endured buying and restoring property in Italy. On our side, we had modern tools like the Internet for instant communications and a restoration team at the other end handling everything for us as part of the purchase agreement. I guess you'd call it a turnkey operation. This included, for example, everything from coordinating with the seller, closing the sale at the notary's office in Calitri, overseeing the renovations/improvements and contractors, connecting utilities, providing basic furnishing, even setting up a postal account to pay recurring electric and water bills. Yes, in Italy the post offices are mini-banks of sorts where you can pay some bills as you monitor things from back in the States via the Internet. It was like being in flight on autopilot. We finally landed just last week when we received photos of the finished product, *Casa della Foritoia*.

Honestly, without the Internet, doing this remotely would be impossible. The local council's vision, their cooperation, and the great development team assembled, were unique and a timely godsend. If we'd attempted this on our own, we would have to have been in Italy watching every step of the process. That is, if we could have ever gotten things going to begin with or even understood the process. Who did we know well enough to take care of things for us? No one! It would have meant putting it off until we were retired and had the time. If we'd tried ourselves, we'd probably be divorced and broke by now, but on the brighter side, our Italian would definitely be better. As a current TV commercial intones, "I got people!"

Our place was in pretty good shape from the start. Old? Yes, indeed. As I've mentioned, over our entry inscribed in the marble jamb is the date '1875' but that was a much later renovation date then the origin of the structure, I'm sure. It goes farther back, as indicated by its name *Casa della Feritoia* – House of the Arrow Slit, as in bow and arrows . . . you certainly don't see those around anymore.

Oh, by the way, I now know what they call this fascination with Italy. It's called Italomania! Tell me, does that come under the *Americans with Disabilities Act?*

March, 2007

5

And No One Clapped

As in many other Italian towns, Calitri closes down for the *riposo* around 1 p.m. each day to awaken again by 4 p.m.. If you are late getting lunch and it gets past one in the afternoon, forget about it. With the renewal of activity in the late afternoon, the pulse of the community continues until roughly 9 p.m.. Around then, establishments close and families come together for their evening meal. Pretty late dining for uninitiated, non-Europeans like us. It is during this five-hour evening interlude that something special happens each and every night in Calitri.

It was an April Sunday evening in Calitri. The main *corso* was closed to traffic as on all such Sunday evenings in full expression of the poetry of the *passeggiata*, a custom where many of the townspeople flood into the street in keeping with an ancient tradition of meeting each other at the end of day and exchanging greetings. How this began, I have no idea and there is nothing comparable to it in America. Families walk arm-in-arm. Groups of ladies, most likely lifelong friends who have enjoyed this promenade since they walked together as children, chat and greet passersby as they make their way.

Some evening strollers, accompanied by older companions, help them along, a bolster to a cane in their companion's other hand. Children buzz through the throngs of people like fireflies and older gentlemen line the benches under the trees as if they were the marshals of a parade. It's something special to see and experience. This particular evening, the *buònasera's* were being traded as if it were Christmas morning and gifts were exchanging hands. People we had only recently met – a waiter, a store-owner, a workman, made the effort to greet us and chat – us with weak Italian and them with unpracticed English.

**9.Watching fireworks during
the passeggiata**

We had only been there a few days by then, but already we felt comfortable with greeting passersby with just a *sera* verses the full-blown *buònasera*.   People instinctively knew we were outsiders, new to this place. It was probably because of my height and the style of the clothes we wore. More likely, it may have been because in all the past litany of *passeggiata*, we'd

10. Fireworks, downtown Calitri

never attended one and therefore stuck out like a Boston fan at a Yankee grudge game in the Broncs!

It was on this particular night of *passeggiata*, while standing in the doorway of *Speedy Pizza*, chatting as best we could in Italian with the owner as we waiting for a pizza, that there was a loud boom, actually an explosion, that hushed any further conversations. Seeing it is normal here to have *bombolla* gas bottles next to your stove, inside your home, my first thought was that somewhere nearby one had exploded. The cacophony continued, however, and as we stepped out into the street, the night sky above the castle overlooking the *Borgo* lit up in a thunderous fireworks display. From the valley floor, far below Calitri, it had to have been a wonderful sight. It was a spectacular display. We learned later, when a crowd of young people, some sporting jester hats, streamed into town from the square outside the town hall and the *Borgo*, that it had something to do with the town's soccer team. Just as a boom had announced the start of this vibrant sky-show, it concluded with an equally loud concussion. It was over as quickly as it had begun. Surprisingly, there was silence among those around us.

As we instinctively applauded in appreciation for what had just occurred, they turned their heads away from the sky to continue their soiree as if nothing had happened. They were silent. Some looked at us because of our response, standing there as we were in the street clapping, still looking skyward as the last flickers of fire faded and the smoke trails dissipated in the night breeze. This reaction on our part must have seemed peculiar to them. Yet, as our eyes met those of a group of nearby women, they took up our expression of thanks and also began to clap. How quickly ideas spread. How quickly Calitri made us feel accepted.

If ever in Calitri, be sure to experience the *passeggiata*. There may even be a fireworks display, if you're lucky. You might even want to clap. Vacations become a part of us, because of the memories they instill . . . Calitri will too!

May, 2007

6

A Book By Its Cover

If you head up *Corso Garibaldi,* one of the main streets in downtown Calitri, pass the *Bar Jolly* and keep going until the street becomes *Corso Italia,* you will come to a sign pointing to the right indicating *Tre Rose.* Take the right into what appears to be a complex of apartment houses, find *#9 Via Sotto Macello* and you've found *Tre Rose!*

It sports a nondescript, quite modest exterior like many of the other jewels in Calitri. No alfresco menu, no chic, flood-lit

11. The Tre Rose
Osteria tiled sign, Calitri

marquee. Forget about valet parking.

Count yourself lucky if you can find a parking space in this family neighborhood. Unlike in the *Borgo*, here people drive and park cars. Honestly, the first time we drove by looking for it, we were unimpressed by its appearance. In fact, we hesitated to stop and give it a try. Only a sign proclaiming *Tre Rose*, some planters, and a street-side gas barbecue grill mark the spot. But for the sign denoting the place, you'd never think it was a restaurant. Be cautioned though, and remember what they say about telling a book from its cover.

Actually, *Tre Rose* is an *osteria*. In years past, the town square, the church and the local *osteria* were the primary meeting places for small-town Italians. It was a tavern or humble restaurant where wine was served along with regional food. It was a place where both rich and poor could intermingle. Here the cultured and un-instructed could sometimes find a way to communicate around a table with a pack of playing cards and a carafe of wine. Today in Calitri it remains much the same. The *osteria* is an Italian institutional tradition.

Back home in the States, we continually hear claims of "authentic regional Italian cuisine", but what exactly is authentic Italian cuisine? Well, one definition is embodied in the *Tre Rose* . . . It's where, in the tiny kitchen, the cooks are clad in white smocks and their hair bedecked in a white shower-cap affair as if they were NASA technicians; It's where one of the owners, now in his 40s has worked in this establishment since he was 17; It's where the walls of the dining area are tiled, beams segment the ceiling and cloth adorns clusters of appealing tables; It's where a TV charms the eye, causing one to glance away from the most pleasing of dinner companions and steal a glimpse at an amazing head-nod shot into the net; It's where a buffet table of calamari, eggplant, zucchini and deep fried smelts, guarded by a phalanx of wine bottles, beckons; and it's where a *vecchio* (old) outside grill roasts steaks and lamb much to the aromatic delight of the neighborhood. And oh yes, it has all got to be in Italy! Such is the local *osteria*—a great place to meet and enjoy the company of Italians you might never encounter in your customary travels as a tourist.

It hasn't an extensive wine list. Just point to what you want, ask for the house wine or if you're lucky, patrons at a neighboring table might just share a bottle of their homemade brew with you. The service, though nowhere as elegant as in some Roman or Neapolitan establishment, is excellent, prompt, and especially congenial. They are as interested in you as you are in them.

12. The Saturday night help yourself buffet at Tre Rose

All that is needed is that spark of initiative on your part to strike up a conversation, no matter how meager your Italian might be. You can be sure they will help you out with that. Its menu, though limited, promises to capture the Italian spirit of making every meal a special occasion. The homemade house pastas, though regular fare, are a special treat for the novice. It was for us. Imagine a bowl of fresh pasta with meat sauce or potato gnocchi, enough for four, for only 3,50 Euros, and so, so good. Shh, don't tell anyone!

Not on the menu one night was an adjacent table of six elderly men. They were all locals and seemingly lifelong friends. We learned that every Saturday night they gathered at the *Tre Rose* for dinner. One was 75 years old, but surprisingly looked 55—could it be the olive oil? All were retired now and *sulle pensioni* (on pensions). Some had worked for years in Germany, because that's where the jobs were at the time, while their families remained behind in Calitri. The most interesting part was that they had their own supply of homemade wine stored at the *Tre Rose* for these weekly occasions! They kindly presented us with one bottle, and when that was downed, we happily accepted another (and I can recall the days when we had a hard time finishing a single bottle of wine!) By then, I could easily attest to the distinctive flavor of the Aglianico grape, local to the region, and from which their wine was made. In particular, I learned that the Aglianico grape is a very tannic grape, which is tamed only by harvesting it as late as possible, often in late October, to ensure full ripeness. When done correctly, it competes with the "big" Sangiovese and Nebbiolo based wines from Tuscany and Piedmont.

Go ahead and capture the Italian spirit of making every

meal a special occasion and try the *Tre Rose*. Be adventurous, walk inside, and surround yourself with the culinary warmth of time-honored cooking, the local spice of *Calitrani* life and the timeless charm of bygone times.

As for the name of this establishment, I'm honestly sitting here wondering to myself why I never inquired as to its origin. Well, next time when the wine begins to flow, I'll be sure to ask.[1]

May, 2007

---

[1]   We were yet new to Calitri at this point. Only later did we discover that *Tre Rose* (Three Roses) was the heraldic symbol of Calitri, seen throughout town on plaques and shields.

13. Tre Rose camaraderie, Calitri

14. Lucia, born, raised, lived, loved and died in Calitri

7

For Lucia

We had the opportunity to meet some of our neighbors quite by happenstance when we visited Calitri. On our first trip, we met an elderly woman who invited us, total strangers, into her home after meeting us in the lane just outside her *Borgo* home.

Lucia had lost much of her physical beauty with the years. She maneuvered using aluminum crutches, the type with the cup supports for your arms—a style I'd always associated with polio victims but soon realized were quite common among the elder citizenry of Calitri. What clearly remained was her strong and beautiful spirit, undiminished over her many years. Although we could barely communicate with one another, we understood what she was trying to tell us, as though through some universal language. We had an unspoken understanding, for example, when she opened her bedroom dresser drawer to proudly display her handmade linens to my wife. These were truly proud possessions from a bygone time.

The room was modest. I recall the *matrimoniale* bed with its great headboard, bedspread and a quilt, most likely also handmade, folded across its foot to, no doubt, ward-off nighttime dampness. Her dresser was bedecked with black and white, filigree-framed pictures recounting episodes in her life. I especially remember one photo of her mustached husband in his finery. These days she slept alone in that bed, since, as she explained, holding his picture, her *marito* was now departed.

She pointed out the window toward a small, roadside church on a nearby ridge, guarded by a solitary pine, which lay down the mountainside and across the pastoral countryside. It is now locked and rarely used. She hesitantly explained that she had been married there many years before. This triggered a question from Maria Elena as to whether Lucia had lived **here** all her life to which she simply replied "no". When my wife inquired further, as to where else she had lived, as we imagined places like Naples or Sorrento, her humble reply brought a smile to our faces. She had also lived a few streets farther down the mountainside beneath the window! Essentially, she had lived in Calitri all her life. Although the outside world undoubtedly changed greatly over this time-span, Calitri and Lucia remained constants, not much altered since the day she'd emerged from that church into the sunlight, the expanse of the Calitri *Borgo* stretched out before her. Most likely it was we who represented change—an influx of mostly English and American ex-patriots yearning for that romantic sense of a quiet place called home in Italia, where you can savor people's friendship and their genuine and spontaneous personalities.

Our lives only crossed paths for all of 15 or 20 minutes. We would have liked to have sustained this new friendship, but Lucia, I'm told, passed away during the winter of 2007. I wish

I'd known her when she was young. I can imagine her climbing the *Path of Cupa* from the fields in the valley below up toward the Castle and into the village on strong limbs, unencumbered by supports, her head full of tomorrows yet to be captured in photos on her dresser.

45

August, 2007

8

Life of Riley Hospitality

Recently I wrote about 'bella Lucia'. It was only days later and not many streets away from Lucia's home that we met Maria and her husband, Vito, as we again explored the maze of streets that comprise the medieval *Borgo* of Calitri.

15. Vito and Maria, Calitri Borgo

We'd stopped just outside a doorway to admire a terra cotta, pot-based garden, which complemented the brick accented doorway and windows of an attractive home. Apparently there are no *terra firma* style gardens in the *Borgo*. At least, we haven't seen any. The door itself sported a sort of pass-through curtain, which if you have been to Italy, you will recall as a series of long dangling fingers stretching from the top of the entryway to the threshold. Some are made from what look like soft but gargantuan fuzzy pipe-cleaners, others are made of long plastic strips. I've no idea what they're called.

16. Two Marias chat about a potted garden, Calitri Borgo

They are quite functional in keeping flying pests out, which by the way, we haven't noticed to be a problem in Calitri, high up as it is. They also serve as an effective shade from sunlight entering the open doorway and heating the house.

As we enjoyed the flower and herb arrangements, Maria emerged from her dangling doorway to join us outside. She had apparently heard us. She was somewhat shorter and older than us. She wore a full-length smock that might also serve as a workaday apron, and wore earrings, a gold necklace and red slippers to match her red sweater top. With the help of an English neighbor, we were introduced, and then talked for a while about her plants as we inspected leaves and flowers. She was proud of her street-side, potted garden. Shortly thereafter, she invited us inside her immaculate home. We got the grand tour. Most noteworthy was her very modern kitchen, complete with a countertop TV, gas range, and built-in dishwasher. You

17. Maria serves us a snack in her kitchen

don't see many of them thereabouts. It wasn't long before she invited us to sit at the kitchen table, and like any mom, soon brought out food and insisted we *mangiare* (eat). Vito soon arrived and offered us his homemade *vino*. Many times I relate my impression of what someone looks like to familiar actors. Vito struck me as a look-alike for William Bendix! Do you remember him from that early American TV sitcom *The Life of Riley*, with his wife Peg and his catch phrase, which become part of the national idiom, "What a revolt-in' development this is!" I fear I may be dating myself.

His wine was in an attractive, clear, octagonal bottle topped with a porcelain stopper permanently fastened to the bottle. It was pure Aglianico, not a blend, and wonderfully satisfying and tasty as we sat around the table in the shade of their kitchen. Vito apparently had a vineyard somewhere nearby in the countryside and produced enough to satisfy their annual needs. I appreciate *vino*-sharing chaps like Vito! I also enjoyed the dried, homemade sausage Maria cut up for us, especially while I imbibed Vito's locally made brew. We laughed and talked, drank and ate in the cool of her pleasant kitchen as RAI TV news backlit the countertop until afternoon had taken hold. Ah, the little *Life of Riley* pleasures in life.

I've always liked and respected older people. While in their presence, there is something about them that has continually fascinated me. Maybe it's their polite manner, rarely manifested these days in my contemporaries. It could be that I enjoy the stories of old times and old ways. Maybe it's just the realization, as I get older myself, that you have to be one tough bird to survive to your geriatric years and beyond. By then, you've earned that 10% coffee discount at *Dunkin Donuts* and an AARP membership! Getting old really isn't for sissies.

When it was time to leave, we got a quick tour of Vito's nearby grotto. In the chilled atmosphere of his hollowed-out, mountainside cellar, the wine we had so enjoyed aged in well-used wooden barrels and demijohns arrayed with plastic tubing and siphons. We left with two 2-liter plastic bottles of last year's excellent product. There was no way we could refuse them but then I didn't want to.

This was one of our first adventures into local *Calitrani* hospitality. Curious, kind, friendly, definitely hard working, hospitable and well meaning, Vito and Maria are wonderful neighbors to have and to get to know better. Contrary to what Riley might say, "What an agreeable development this is!"[1]

September, 2007

---

[1]   My friend Vito passed away in the Spring of 2014.

9

Cinderella Cat

We were getting used to our home in Calitri. We had visited for six days in the spring but upon returning in October, we had a full two weeks to relax, settle in, and explore more of the local area. It wasn't long before we became familiar with things. We knew where to throttle the shower for that just right temperature, we knew the correct amount of *Illy* ground coffee for a morning pot, we knew which switches controlled which lights. Even the voices on *Radio Carina* didn't sound so foreign after a while. We felt like we were home.

We also had time to get familiar with some of the newly-opened restaurants in town. One of these, a special gem, was the *La Gatta Cenerentola* (Cinderella Cat), just a few streets below us in the medieval *centro storico* of Calitri. I didn't get the reasoning behind the name but that doesn't matter—the food, cheeses and wines there were wonderful.

How should I describe it? The *Cat* is located in a grotto, a hollowed-out subterranean cave dug deep into the hillside on *Via Tozzoli*. If it could recount its history to us, it would undoubtedly be a tale of sheltering animals, wine making,

**18. Sign over the door of the
Cinderella Cat, Calitri Borgo**

aging cheeses, and curing *prosciutto* along with sundry other uses spanning hundreds of years. In way of testimony to these bygone times, suspension rings are still visible in the ceiling.

There was, however, no earlier use quite as elegant as today's application. Elegance begins at the entrance. It's like walking in from a time centuries earlier, denoted by the medieval passageway just outside, right into the 21st century. A light embedded in the stone pavement at the doorway marks the transition. Advertised as a *Taverna del Gusto* (Tavern of Taste), it had approximately 28 seats. The entire establishment occupied one long, subterranean space divided by a stone archway into two seating areas. The smaller space to the rear was slightly raised and offered more privacy and intimacy. Off to one side in an adjoining annex was a kitchen, demarcated by a brightly colored entryway. There isn't a bad seat in the place but who would care—you're in Italy, aren't you? The owners undoubtedly remodeled the space extensively and their efforts were bountifully rewarded. Original stone—walls, archways, newly tiled floors, attractive seating, indirect lighting. Even the entrance door and a window accented with terra cotta roof tiles lend the dining space an air of mystery and privacy.

The layout isn't the only interior detail worth noting. Decorative accents and colors add just the right ambiance. Illuminated wall niches host displays of beckoning wines such as *Taurasi Terredoro* and *Mier Irpinia Aglianico*, while additional recesses, including some displays on the floor toward the rear of the dining area, shelter little stashes of additional *vini*. The *Cat* is adorned with rich decorative strokes. Enameled yellow and red radiators flank some of the wall space. Very bright and colorful greens and reds liven the space further, while earth tones from stone after stone help temper the decorative enthusiasm and remind us of the past and where we are.

These weren't the only interior details. The *Cat* also features a large photo composed of three adjacent panels, depicting the *Borgo* cityscape cascading down the mountainside, each colored in separate pastel hews of blue, green, and red. This was meaningfully symbolic to me. Nothing encapsulates the complete *Cat* experience like this image, displayed as it is on its own rough plaster backdrop as if in a place of honor— juxtaposing the distant past with the contemporary. The panel is the modern equivalent of the painted murals on similar walls, not too many miles distant, in Pompeii and Herculaneum. To me it is a fitting tribute to the traditions of Calitri and the hard life of its earlier inhabitants.

But what about the fare? After all, we were there to eat.

At that time, the menu featured over twenty selections, not including the wines of which there were 14 varieties to choose from. For starters, there were the ever-present Italian antipasto favorites of *tagliere dei formaggi* and *salumi*. We enjoyed these one night, and could have made a meal of them. In fact, I think we did, only to be complemented by *dolce* of chocolate cake accented with a liqueur.

Salads of *mozzarella caprese, rucola e scaglie di pecorino* and another named *insalatina variopina* preceded the various types of *bruschetta*. The evening's first plate was a delicious pasta dish of freshly made *gnocchi*, while the *secondo* was a slab of roasted veal. These entrees vary from evening to evening. Additional cheese specialties (since the Cheese Grotto is next door) for added variety and a bit of local flare included:

>*Tortino di Caciocavallo all'aceto Balsalmico*
>
>*Scamorza Arrostita*
>
>*Caciocavallo di Grotto Arrostito*
>
>*Ricottina calda con Marmellata di Frutta*
>
>*Treccia Calitrana*

As for the wines, we stuck with *vini rossi* and began with the *Taurasi Terredora* mentioned earlier—very smooth with an old world flavor and later tried an *Aglianico doc Mier Vini*—again smooth with a little bite when it had gone past the tongue. Better than food? Decide for yourself. The prices are very reasonable, and along with the excellent food, wines and service will bring us back again and again. Which reminds me, our server was the lovely Maria Teresa, herself almost feline in black attire.

I'd say the *Cinderella Cat* is already one of Calitri's top dining establishments, although being a *taverna*, it has limited selections. For wine and cheese, however, it has no equal, or at least we haven't found it yet. Any limitations are more than overcome by the quality and presentation of the fare. A rags to riches story like the Cinderella story we all know? I certainly hope so.

In addition to the food and wine, there is the company you share. Groups of two and four came and went as we lingered to savor not only our food, but our limited time there. In fact, on our first evening, at one point I joined a nearby table of four men. One gentleman, the owner of a nearby cheese grotto, took us on a tour of his cheese aging cave and from there on to another of his projects, this one inside a labyrinth of subterranean grottos. The latter focused on *prosciutto* and was still under development. It will be the subject of a future story, I'm sure. Which brings me back to that image of Calitri I'd seen showcased in the *Cat's* stone cavern, that had inspired my imagination to speculate on what other jewels await the adventurous on this mountainside called Calitri. Unlike our shower and coffee pot, will we ever be totally familiar with the workings and magic places of Calitri? With much to anticipate, I certainly hope not!

November, 2007

10

Vertically Challenged

I'm tall, over six feet. Because of this attribute, I've enjoyed both advantages and disadvantages throughout my life. In grammar school for instance, I was always seated at the back of the classroom. Luckily I had good eyesight. In 'ranks', where we lined up to go to or return from recess, I was always at the back of the file. In my school, it was some sort of obsession with well aligned and proportioned appearance that went hand-in-hand with boys to one side and girls to the other. Today, we carry it over into well manicured lawns, obedient shrubbery, even to the extent

**19. Author picking grapes,
Calitri countryside**

that our underwear is neatly folded and aligned in our dresser drawers with socks to the front! In high school, tall as I was, I was the center on the basketball team. In the service when I flew, I always had to bottom my seat to avoid the canopy. In the business' cubical world, I could see over the partitions, and with that advantage, could avoid collisions with much shorter hot coffee-toting associates. Most of this was beyond my control, something I just had to live with. My height, however, didn't help in the least when it came to picking grapes recently in Calitri.

That's right, picking grapes. Most people go to Italy to see its historic sites or maybe to attend a cooking school. Not us. In the fall we align our visits with the *vendemmia* (grape harvest) season. I harbored pre-conceived images of Lucille Ball from that now famous 1956 TV episode where, while on a trip to Italy, she crushed grapes with her bare feet. Have you seen it? It's out there on Internet if you'd like to have a laugh.

I knew a Lucy type adventure wouldn't be the case for us—times had changed. Instead of purple stained feet, all we could expect, at most, were possibly purple stained hands. To prevent this, we were offered latex gloves and advised to not squeeze too hard! If you were adept at this sort of thing (and had longer fingernails than I), you could quickly snip a clump of grapes from the vine with your fingers. In my case, I used some garden shears while Maria Elena used scissors to clip off the grape bunches, being careful not to snip in the blind and clip a finger. I was wearing some old walking shoes and workpants, which I planned to leave behind in Calitri. Maria

Elena donned a pair of high-top rubber boots and off she went with her manicured nails and bucket in hand. We were a Hansel and Gretel pair for sure, leaving nothing behind but footprints in the mud.

The actual day of the harvest had been postponed a few days because of weather. We had had both rain and light snow the days before, but harvest day dawned bright and crisp. We awoke with smiles in anticipation of events, and soon were out in the countryside about 3-4 miles from Calitri as the crow flies, actually just inside of Basilicata. The scene was a rustic palette—the hills undulated in a verdant tapestry scattered with distant rooftops, forests, newly plowed fields, fog-bound valleys, all of it topped-off with an azure sky. It was a day beckoning for a fall harvest.

This tradition had gone on for centuries, and now, throughout the Calitri *Borgo*, you could hear the scouring sound of dry *pungitopo* bushes cleaning the insides of fermentation barrels and smell the fragrance of newly crushed grapes as grotto after grotto once again came alive as mini oenology laboratories. Each had its own family method of vinification. In fact, Italy was once called *Oenotria*, the "Land of Wine," because of its Mediterranean sunshine, mountain air currents, and rich soil that fostered the growth of healthy grapevines. The crushing, stirring and snap-crackle-pop sound of fermentation of the newly harvested grape crop was underway in street after street throughout the *centro storico*. Just about every *buongiorno* resulted in a sample of the new year's brew, sometimes going as far as the offer of a bottle of last year's creation, since practically everyone participated in this national pastime.

Here was a practice steeped in family tradition. Our particular *famgilia* consisted of mother, Lucia; her son, Antonio; her sister-in-law, Angela; Angela's daughter Giuseppina; myself and Maria Elena. The six of us had the production of two vineyards to gather. Fortunately, we were in the hands of experts. Lucia had been doing this since she was three. In those bygone days, she had to walk the miles to and from these

**20. Maria Elena harvesting
grapes, Calitri countryside**

same fields. Learning traditions definitely begins early, if they are to last a lifetime.

New to all this, we had much to learn and we soon did. Italy is the largest producer of wines in the world, has more types of vines planted than any other country, and produces the greatest range of distinctive wines. It's also the world's largest wine exporter. We were definitely in the right place.

Because of the muddy conditions, it wasn't possible to kneel down while picking. Oh, I guess we could have, but I didn't want to deal with the consequences. It would have been convenient, however. Instead, I had to stoop and bend to reach the fruit-laden parts of the vines, which to me seemed to grow closest to the ground. Getting at them, after a while, became a challenge for someone as tall as myself. Here, there was no advantage to being tall.

The constant bending soon took its toll on my weak back muscles, but what the heck, this is what we had come for.

We were picking Aglianico grapes, a major varietal in this part of Italy, where Italian wines first started. History says they originated in Greece. I've read that the name may be a corruption of *Vitis Hellenica*, Latin for "Greek vine." Even in early Roman times it was the principal grape of the famous *Falernian* wine often mentioned in Roman literature and even nowadays in modern day historical novels (try the wonderful Colleen McCullough, *Masters of Rome* series).

Collecting the grapes into our buckets went smoothly. We sang songs as we went along, row following row of vines, like honey-bees in search of nectar. Our offering to the buzz went like this familiar tune composed by Harry Warren and lyricist Jack Brooks, made famous by Dean Martin . . .

"When the moon hits your eye like a big pizza pie
That's amore
When the world seems to shine like you've had too much wine
That's amore
Bells will ring ting-a-ling-a-ling, ting-a-ling-a-ling

The day had turned warm. We had shed layers of clothing and in about four hours or so, had filled the larger buckets in the truck from our individual pails. Italians usually drink wine with food, hardly ever just by itself, but after we were done with the harvest the *famiglia* celebrated alongside the truck, now overflowing with our purple treasure trove, with a toast to this year's harvest and shared *salutes* with cupfuls of last year's product.

After picking some wild chicory, exploring a ruined farmhouse, and stopping by a farm for a short visit with family friends, we returned to Calitri where the celebration continued over a fine meal already being prepared by Pasqualina, Antonio's sister. Ah, the pleasures of grape harvesting for both the tall and short.

It was only later that we got around to crushing the grapes in a shed out back. A feed auger similar to an old style ringer washer or the rotating drums of a pencil sharpener, only much larger, did the job. It straddled an open-topped, wooden barrel used for fermentation. Antonio had long ago replaced the typical crank handle on the device with an electric motor, which made short work of the entire crushing process. We fed buckets of grape clusters into the auger where they were systematically crushed, along with their stems, within seconds. We took care beforehand to remove any leaves, damaged grapes, and any other debris that may have been gathered along with the grapes. The resulting crushed mass undergoes fermentation all together.

So what is fermentation really? Well, simply put, it occurs when yeast cells eat the grape's natural sugar and produce alcohol as a byproduct. It's where that 12 or 13% alcohol by volume on a label comes from. Yeast, indigenous to the vineyards, was already present on the grapes, sometimes even visible in a grape's powdery appearance. These natural yeasts carry out the fermentation, miraculously transforming the juice into wine. Unfortunately for busy yeast cells, alcohol is poisonous to them and in the end the alcohol will kill the yeast, putting a stop to fermentation. It turns out, however, that yeast cells are smarter than we might think. Addicted to sugar as they are, and unable to stop devouring it, they have to do something special if they're to stay alive for as long as possible. When they sense that their sugar supply is getting low (or is it when the alcohol level gets high?), they start sprouting 'hairs'. After swimming around for a while, these now hairy yeast cells get tangled up with each other and eventually get heavy enough to sink to the bottom of the barrel. The cells in the upper layer of this bottom sediment effectively act as life guards, protecting their brethren with their own bodies. This semi-martyrdom allows other cells to stay alive longer, even in a poisonous alcoholic environment. Though there isn't much to see, there is certainly a load of chemistry going on in that barrel.

Once fermentation begins, the grape skins are pushed to the surface by carbon dioxide gases, also released in the fermentation process. This accounted for the snap-crackle-pop we could hear close by the open fermentation barrel. This surface layer of skins and other solids is the source of the tannins and needs to be mixed through the liquid a few times a day. This is traditionally done by stomping through the barrel, not with your feet, but with a multi-pronged stick.

Antonio allows about ten days for fermentation. While the technology of winemaking can be very complicated, here I thought it was quite straightforward with traditional ways of doing things well in play. According to our personal oenologist, after fermentation is completed, the filtered liquid will be transferred to oak casks for further flavor enhancement. This allows the wine time to spawn greater complexity and character. We wouldn't be there for the spawning and character building, but gladly promised to return to savor the finished product on a return visit.

From this experience, I now have my own theory about why Italians are themselves vertically challenged, being in general, people of short stature that they are. Natural selection, limited dietetic choices in the past, a rogue designer gene or two . . . I haven't the slightest idea how it may have come about, but I do know being built closer to the ground sure helps when it comes to harvesting grapes! My suggestion? Next year, get those grapes to grow along the tops of the trellises instead of the bottoms of the vines. Even growing in the middle would be helpful. That way nature could help out nature and avoid the compensatory doses of *Advil* needed to put things right again. Or maybe I should quit with the grapes entirely and become an olive harvest specialist instead, something more my size but I fear even more strenuous.

Humor aside, this was a wonderful experience and gave us a firsthand appreciation of what it really takes to produce just one bottle of this liquid sunshine. That, along with the camaraderie of our newfound Italian *famiglia*—where we are called *zio e zia* (uncle and aunt)—and their centuries-old traditions, made a very special memory to take pleasure from long into the future. We want to do it again and again and again and that my friend is the short and tall of it.

The promise of little pleasures like these is as enchanting as ever in Calitri. It's no wonder a dreamer and romantic like me continues to love this most idyllic hideaway.

December, 2007

11

Shaving Cream Serendipity

As I've gotten older, that being only recently mind-you, I've changed my shaving habits. Not quite your normal mid-life crisis material but still a substantial change in habit for me. You see, up to this point in my life, I've used an electric razor. In the slower pace of time I sense in Italy, I've switched to shaving cream and a hand razor. Is it the 'in a hurry' American pace falling victim to the influences of a more laidback, less hectic lifestyle? I suspect so. I just enjoy shaving this way now. In the past, I'd sometimes shave as I drove to work, sometimes even at my desk. While

21. The Statue of the Immigrant, Calitri

some might have an extra shirt or tie in their desk drawer, I had an electric razor. It saved me 5-10 minutes—damning testimony to a fast-paced, time-conscious lifestyle indeed.

It followed then that when we were last in Calitri, I needed to get some shaving cream since it was easier to get it there than go through the hassle of carrying it with me on the flight from home. It so happened then that one day, as we leisurely explored the ancient *Borgo*, I stopped in at a shop on *Via Concezione* looking for some shaving cream. It was a very old establishment, passed down in the family from father to son. Situated at a major intersection of streets made it somewhat centrally located in the lower village, no doubt attributing to its continued existence. Inside I met Tommaso, the current proprietor. He was a medium build, middle-aged man with a receding hairline, moving to gray, with lips prone to a congenial smile. Even in mid-October he wore a quilted, insulated jacket and sweater to ward off the chill of his shop, which, cave-like, stretched back into the coolness of the hillside.

His shop-space was lined with tall cabinets and shelves extending almost to the ceiling, many with long glass door inserts to display products. Even the floor was dense with sales items. I recall cleaning products and soaps mostly. It brought back memories of my childhood five-and-dime store, something long since torn down but still remembered for its long, creaky wooden-planked floor and the smell of freshly made popcorn as it percolated from a suspended pot.

A long counter and a corner wall close to the door carved out a space behind the counter where Thomas sat during his

**22. Tommaso at the counter of
his shop, Calitri Borgo**

day's vigil. He had a computer back there with him, which undoubtedly offered some relief and helped keep his hours occupied. He produced the aerosol shaving cream I'd asked for and we talked a while longer, right out into the street. It was then that he led me, a few doors and turns away, to meet his neighbor and apparent friend, Fulvio. I recall Thomas escorting me to a nondescript entry adjacent to a cozy *vicolo* (alley) patio arrayed with chairs and succulent plants and a single blooming rose. Inside I met Fulvio.

Fulvio Moscaritolo, another baby boomer, was born six days before me in 1946. That was in Mirabella Eclano, a hilltop town located northwest of Avellino, not far from the prime Campanian wine country of Taurasi. Fulvio appears to be a serious soul. My few-minute impression of him was that some inner drive ruled his temperament and channeled his creativity. In solidarity with other young *Irpinian* artists, he struck out in the 1960's in search of new forms of artistic expression. His quest led him to a lifetime of expression through cubism, then modernism, and on to today's social consciousness over the plight of man and the consequences of invention on nature. Clean-shaven, his dark, arched eyebrows contrasted with his thin graying hair. Professorial, I'd call him.

What especially distinguishes this *Calitriani* is that he is an extraordinary artist who works in multiple mediums. Fulvio is an architect of the mind who builds eternal beauty and wonder from inspiration and thought. His studio, right there in Calitri, is called the *Art Institute of Calitri*. As a renowned ceramist, painter and sculptor, he has participated in numerous exhibitions and received significant awards and recognition, among them the title of *International Contemporary Ceramicist of Florence*. Several of his works appear in public and private collections.

In fact, one of his creations is on display in downtown Calitri in the park where *Via Gagliano* diverges from *Corso Garibaldi*. It is an exceptional example of his sculpting abilities entitled *La Statua dell' Emigrante* (Statue of the Immigrant). It was commissioned by the very same person depicted in the composition, Antonio Zazzarino. For those of you not familiar with it, it is a life-size bronze depiction of Antonio who, in the 1950's, departed Calitri and his family to seek his fortune in Venezuela. He was a shoemaker by trade, which is hinted at by various scenes involving shoemaking on each side of the statue's base. There you find four deep relief plaques, beautifully busy with detail, depicting scenes of his departure, some with the village as backdrop.

His story has a happy ending, for he indeed found success in the shoe business and in his new life with Marie, an émigré like himself whom he met and married in Caracas. The sculpture portrays him as a young man, his expression resolute, gazing off into the distance and carrying all his possessions with him: a rope-lashed suitcase (actually made of paper at the time) in hand, a canteen on his hip, and a bundle under his arm—a simple testament to a man with a dream, captured in time at the moment Antonio, along with his dream, first set out, alone, from Calitri.

Fulvio's studio on the sunbathed hillside of Calitri was vibrant that morning with color and the illumination of a pleasant October day. Tiny dust particles danced in sheets of brilliant sunlight. The light was amplified further by the whitewashed walls of his studio. There, as everywhere, sunlight is meaningful whether you are an artist or an average Joe. Daily, the sun has risen to begin its pageant across the sky and eventually, one day, someone called it time.

Ah yes, time, that slippery thing. From the time we first set foot on the floor until we once again lift them our feet into

23. Fulvio in his art gallery, Calitri

our beds, we follow paths of daily routine. Our routines are as complex, hurried, or as simple as each of us makes them. Time passes slowly in smooth rivulets or abruptly, in a rush, and disjointed, as when a cellular burst demands our immediate attention. This concept of time seeks to manage our lives and regulate our actions. It moves in sync with the same sun that storms through Fulvio's windows, filling his rooms, illuminating his canvas, and inspiring his creative invention. The same sun, in time, also floods a nearby vineyard to infuse liquid energy into its grapes. Still, that same sun lights and timestamps our way as we go about our daily routines, be they fast-paced or relaxed, signified by shaving cream.

The first room of Fulvio's studio, by the entry, was his creative space with worktables, supplies, easels, sketches, works half done and others just begun. An adjacent, larger room presented finished works spanning his artistic repertoire. Displayed here were metal sculptures, oil paintings, and terracotta and enameled pieces that convincingly blurred the boundaries between painting and sculpture. Close by the window I even spied a scale model of his *La Statua dell' Emigrante*, right down to the detail of its base reliefs.

The explosive breadth of representative sculptures showcased there made this annex of the studio seem as cluttered as Tommaso's store. Large, small, delicate, invasive, everywhere—many were of a traditional religious theme but also included were large, modernistic disk-shaped wall plaques, abstract creations, a human torso, excursions into oriental themes, even a horse's head, which triggered in my thoughts images of *The Godfather*, though I knew that was not the intent. The range of artistic expression was exciting. It was like visiting an art dealer, where the works of many artists are arrayed, but in this instance the excitement came from the realization that these works all sprang from a single man's creative talent. I wondered how, day after day, when Fulvio first unlocked his studio, how he'd decide in which medium to begin his day, on what subject. Would it be with paint, torch, brush, clay, wax, hammer, canvas, or paper?

I'm no art critic, yet focusing on Fulvio's painting style alone, which I thoroughly enjoy, it struck me as a cubist combination of Dali with a touch of Picasso. Those that I saw, typically contained multiple discrete elements overlapping and otherwise interacting with each other to form an intricate composite. One particular painting was especially complex with social symbolism. It depicted a naked woman afloat in a lily pond. The distance from her head to toes spanned a space (or was the span one of time?) at first

24. Lady in the Lily Pond, Calitri Borgo

pristine then extended on to one of discarded trash.

Its exact meaning… Purity to corruptive ruin? Harmony verses violence? Each beholder will have to infer for themselves. Another of Fulvio's paintings, which appeared not yet completed, again centered on a floating nude. In this instance, she floated adjacent to a rowboat, her hair adrift in the current, to me reminiscent of how a modern Shakespeare might depict tragic Ophelia. There are others—an abundance of images to fill your mind with reflection, looking for the illumination of interpretation.

If you are ever in need of a work of art to complement your space, accompany you in your life's journey, or are just in need of some shaving cream and a congenial chat, be sure to seek out Fulvio and Tommaso. Theirs is a different world, one where the sun and its offspring, time, have a different meaning and metronome from someone like myself who, though recently begun to reform, still worries about how to shave minutes, here and there, throughout the day. Look for them in Calitri, where one man sees great worth in taking time to lock up his shop and run off with a stranger to introduce a friend, and where another takes time to transfer his thoughts into something which can effect eternity.

January, 2008

12

The Coffee Wizard of Calitri

How imperceptible some things can be. A flower on a wall of flowers, or the *Where's Waldo* in a crowd of people. In this instance, however, this is a misnomer and the farthest you can get from the truth. It's easy to find Waldo because he is really Mario, and his domain is *Mario's Caffé*.

You can't miss it in the mountaintop village of Calitri, it being the only cafe in *Piazza della Repubblica* at the eastern end of *Corso Matteotti*. Separated only by the width of the tunnel (ordered built by *Il Duce*, I'm told), that admits you to the *Borgo*, it sits adjacent to the Town Hall, itself a former Benedictine monastery. Its location makes it a magnet for the comings and goings of just about everyone doing business with the town or passersby.

I like to spend time in *Mario's Caffé*, at least for some part of my day. After all, this is Italy and I'm pinch me, I may be dreaming, really there. Later on, when I am a continent away, back home once again at work, it will seem like it was a dream. Mario's is also very convenient for me, since I pass by as I make my way in and out of the ancient labyrinth of

**25. Barista Mario at his
station in Mario's Cafe, Calitri**

mountainside homes, which we call home. I enjoy stopping in every morning, early, on my way to run some errand while Maria Elena is still asleep. Even when I've nowhere special to go, I'll still walk over. I need strong doses of the atmosphere found there, as pungent as the coffee dripping from its hissing and frothing monstrosity of a coffee machine. Mario runs it as efficiently as the Wizard of Oz had behind his curtain, only here, he's out in the open pulling the levers on his red *La Cimbali* coffee machine. His broad smile accompanies each cup he passes over to you. Forget about a *panini* and the like, this place is strictly for drinks, mainly coffee, the espresso kind. In the morning you can get a *corneto* (think croissant) as a chaser with your coffee if you'd like, but not much more.

Along with Mario you will find Daniela, his wife, but they're not usually together. She takes over the operation when the *Caffè* reopens after *il riposino pomeridiano* (the afternoon nap), around 4 p.m.. I don't know Daniela as well, being as I am, a morning customer.

Outside, the jigsaw puzzle of parked cars doesn't hinder access in the least. Inside there isn't much, just the entire town in the course of a day. I invest one Euro, but my return is hundred fold. With a cup of cappuccino, which Mario expertly brews for me and tops off with sprinkled chocolate, I get a dash of town gossip and politics, a smidgen of talk of births and deaths, I'm stuffed with statistics on who won which football game, saturated with news and weather, and steeped in the presence of everyone who happens to pass through. All you need to do is introduce yourself, if Mario hasn't already done so for you. At times, I've met my accountant, the local Baron, architects, town bureaucrats, laborers working in the *Borgo* and neighbors. It seems the cafe knows no social declension.

I think our bedroom just down the street is bigger than the entire cafe. In fact, I'm certain it is. A long counter extends a handful of meters from a modest glass wall, which also encloses the front door, all the way to a rear stone wall. The smooth surface of the granite-like countertop is strewn with assorted items, which from time-to-time may vary, for example: from a collection jar for the child of some local distressed family, to leaflets announcing the approaching Montello chestnut festival, to a fabulous mobile phone sale somewhere.

Mario's is also noticeably a stand up place. Most patrons stand alongside the counter, in a cluster by the coffee machine. No need to purchase a ticket first before ordering, as you would in an *Autogrill* out on the *autostrada*. Here, Mario does it all from his tiny command center in the far corner flanked by the stone wall, counter and the mirrored shelving behind him lined with aperitifs. A few white plastic lawn chairs are stacked by a single table in the opposite corner. There you will find the current edition of *La Repubblica* and, if you're lucky, *La Gazzetta Sportiva.* I pull out a chair from the stack whenever I plan to stay a while.

On one morning visit, I happened to meet Nazzareno, a retired, Italian, Lieutenant Colonel enjoying his morning espresso. By the way, just as that movie states, "There's no crying in baseball"[1], there is equally no sipping with espresso! Italians handle it just like they're doing shots. It was early fall and still warm to me, yet my ex-military acquaintance had already donned a winter parka, cinched his neck around with a scarf and topped himself off with a cap. No doubt this was his uniform of the day against the advancing elements. He occupied one of the chairs.

We got through introductions and on hearing I was a former pilot, he recounted how, as a young boy during WWII, he'd seen shiny American bombers up close. In 1943, he worked at the Foggia Airfield in Amendola, Puglia, to the north of Calitri. Soon afterward, he watched as lumbering B-17 Flying Fortresses from the 15th Air Force, with big Ys high up on their tails, took-off and hopefully returned from their daring, costly, daylight missions to strike targets like those in the Ploiesti oil fields of Romania, just north of Bucharest.

-----

1   *A League of Their Own* [Motion picture]. (1992). Columbia TriStar Home Video.

Later in his life, he explained, he'd become an anti-aircraft artillery officer and in evidence proudly produced a commemorative medallion attached to his keychain. I was pleased we had never met professionally, in anger. This venue, were we could talk of aircraft and war over coffee, was far more agreeable. Mario, who keeps a supply of aviation literature behind the counter to occupy any time freed-up between rounds of coffees, is an aviation buff of sorts and with me being a former military pilot, the company and nostalgic conversation are always just right.

Then there was the time I remarked about a Vespa calendar on the cafe wall. I like *Vespa* scooters, and hope to one day own one. These particular calendar prints, in each beautiful monthly installment, also came with very attractive ladies on or next to the bikes. I must admit, they resembled pin-ups; the sort you might find painted on the nose-cheek of a formidable bomber or on a calendar in a mechanic's lair, just above his workbench. In this instance, however, each was very discreet, tastefully done, not décolleté at all. Typical of fine Italian style.

As my High School English teacher used to preach long ago, "Write like you are designing a bathing suit . . . make it long enough to cover the subject but short enough to still be interesting!" Ah, those prints in the language of seductive Vargas-like art did the work of a thousand words. The year was not over, but on my comment, barista Mario transformed into humanitarian Mario and without hesitation removed and offered me his cafe's calendar. It now hangs over my workbench back here in the States. It doesn't matter how far out of date it becomes. I'm not using it to keep track of days or months. Instead, it serves as a classic testament to Vespa, Italian beauty, and Mario's generosity. I mention this only because this act of generosity is so typical, not only of Mario but of the citizenry of Calitri as a whole, always kind, willing to drop anything and help out whenever needed.

Looking for fancy or chic? Not at Mario's, for this is real Italia without some imitation wizard or veil separating you from reality, where the people are geared down a notch and life gets lived with panache. If past is prologue to the future, I should be back there soon, sipping Mario's brew with gusto and sopping up that true Italian atmosphere in *Mario's Caffé*. Go ahead, pull up a chair and join me.

February, 2008

13

Spelunking Calitri

Ever read the James Michener epic novel, *The Source?* If you haven't, be sure to read it someday, for it's a fascinating story. It is a sweeping chronology centered on a fictional mound of dirt in Israel. They call them *Tels.* It's said that a keen poker player relies on physical tells, those reactions and habits of other players, to hint at something about their opponent's hand. Equivalently, a mound of dirt can hint at something from what lies below. The novel begins with an archeological dig down to the very bedrock beneath the *Tel.* Unearthed at various levels along the way are artifacts going back 12,000 years. As only Michener can, he then uses each item to spin a tale about how they came to be there, beginning with the oldest relic from the bottom of the dig. He weaves his story upward, employing each excavated discovery in the narrative, to eventually reach the surface, representative of the present day. As you might imagine, it's a long imaginative saga indeed, yet mesmerizing in its historical scope nonetheless. Surprisingly, we had a similar mesmerizing experience deep beneath the streets of Calitri. There are many Calitris. I'd like to describe one, how we got to be there and of our resulting adventure of discovery.

We had just departed the *Cinderella Cat Taverna*. It was late, around closing time actually. Along with us where Donna, a fellow foreign Calitri homeowner, and her sister, Michelle. We were accompanied by four local men I had met that same evening in the *Cat*. This group of businessmen, no-doubt partners to some degree, had moments earlier taken me to a cheese grotto a few doors away. Inside, it was amazing to find hundreds of tear-drop shaped cheeses suspended in

**26. Caciocavallo cheese curing
in the cheese grotto**

midair, reminiscent of bats dangling from a cave ceiling. Pairs of *caciocavallo* cheeses were linked together with a cord. In saddle-bag fashion they were draped over an arrangement of motley timbers suspended just beneath the ceiling. Elsewhere, larger hatbox-sized *pecorino* cheeses shared floor to ceiling shelves. As an artist might lavishly smother his canvas in paint, here, a coating of mold enveloped everything. Nature's hand thus encouraged the cheese to gradually age. It was a sight to behold as the muted illumination of low wattage electric fixtures, mounted here and there, softened the darkness.

Also on display, arrayed in the grotto's entry-room, was an antique olive press. It guarded direct access to where, farther back in the depths of this hillside cave, the cheese rinds took on their gray, blotchy outer skins of mold. The press was a mechanical affair with three ponderous stone roller-wheels arrayed around a central pivot point. They lay within a large, metal, vat-like vessel, and once again seemed poised for the arrival of some bygone olive harvest. No doubt these rollers had made their monotonous rounds over the oily fruit thousands and thousands of times in the past. Now, corrosion encrusted its structure just as the mold gripped the cheeses.

Returning to the *Cat*, I collected the girls who had just finished their sumptuous chocolate desserts and together we moved on down *Via Giuseppe Tozzoli* in the wee hours of the new day. In the private darkness after midnight, we were hostage to the shadows, the towering stone walls to either side of us and the anticipation of what our new friends intended to show us. Angelo, Vincenzo, Luigi and Giuseppe had broached the idea that as a complement to the cheese grotto, they now wanted to show us another of their projects, this one still in the works. It was planned to soon open as a *prosciutto* grotto. Instead of hanging cheeses, I envisioned hams in mid air! Whoever said, "When pigs fly?"

Exactly how we got there, where we turned, and on which

streets we traveled, I do not recall. It may have been the late hour, the darkness, or a general lack of street signs, but I suspect it was more easily explained by the *vino* we all had enjoyed. It must have been a sight though, almost a harlequin parade, as the eight of us moved through the *Borgo*, reveling in the take-your-breath-away *buono cucina* (good food) of the *Cinderella Cat*, the metamorphosis underway in the cheese grotto, arm-in-arm with the expectant conversation of what we would see next.

Eventually we stopped before a bulky weather-worn door. One of our guides produced a very large key and proceeded to make entry. Inside, in the unlit dimness of the room, we could just make out its blank stoic interior. The room was empty as was the rest of this old home. It lay bare, waiting to be refinished as, undoubtedly, it had experienced many times in the past; its previous inhabitants, some ashes, others scattered to the four winds in other homes, in other places. But this was not our destination, only a portal. The key and this room were simply the means of entry to the maze that lay far below. Maneuvering by flashlight, we rounded a corner and proceeded to descend a stairway. It wasn't quite through a looking glass or wardrobe dramatic but we nevertheless had entered another realm.

Starting at the top, we worked our way down, not into some Israeli *Tel*, but into the bowels of Calitri itself. Down, down, and still farther down we were led. How far we eventually descended was difficult to determine. The stairs worked their magic, however, and proved to be a gateway to the past, for we eventually emerged into a series of connected caverns. The as yet vacant rooms, faintly lit and stretching on as they did, room after room, sustained a mood of quietude and privileged emptiness. Thus began our moments in the underworld.

Angelo, who spoke English the best of our hosts, was now our personal guide. Topped with a baseball cap and sporting a puffy, insulated blue vest, he played the part well, looking quite official in his white shirt and tie. The only thing missing was a hand punch to validate tickets, if we had any. Unlike the rooms above, here it was evident that much work had already

27. A view deeper into the Borgo underworld, Calitri

been expended to restore these primal spaces. New bricked walkways were in place. Even the temperature, deep down as we appeared to be, beneath Calitri, was accommodating. We began our exploration at a large circular glass insert in the floor.

Hesitantly, standing on it, we had a glimpse of passageways and tunnels still farther below. It was indeed a honeycombed hive of burrows. Even the walls and ceiling around us had a uniform honey color. On closer inspection, their surfaces, streaked with sedimentary layers, had a sandy consistency. Beautiful, newly-made stone and brick masonry arches served as structural reinforcements here and there and especially around the passageways between rooms. I appreciate stone work, and always marvel at the combined utility and beauty of such things. The indirect lighting on the stonework added a kind of timeless quality to the chambers.

Angelo pointed out a pipe, half buried in the wall, which guided rainwater into a natural cistern still farther below us. This arrangement had supplied water to not only human occupants, but also to their work animals, which once shared these spaces with them. This became apparent when he pointed to a discolored area of the ceiling and then asked us to guess what might have caused it. Well, none of us was successful and a thousand guesses wouldn't have improved our chances. We learned that these darkened patches were not soot, as we had guessed, but were gradually created over a long period of time from the heat generated from decomposing animal manure piled high under that very spot.

In what had clearly been and would again soon be a kitchen space, we inspected an antique *fornacella* stove that historically doubled as a fireplace. Included in the circular holes in the tiled top of the *fornacella* were three copper pots that could be separately heated from individual fireboxes. Nearby was a stone sink, unmistakably hand hewn. The cleft marks from the chisel of some unknown mason were still evident, not unlike those on an unfinished *Buonarroti* statue you'd find in the *Galleria dell'Accademia* in Florence.

As if soaring above this chiseled basin was a magnificent bronze dragon-headed water spigot. There were also limited signs of modernism about. These included an electric meat slicer expecting its due, some stainless steel racks awaiting their hind quarters, and a small gas stove, doubtlessly installed to supplement the *fornacella*.

28. Prosciutto grotto kitchen stove, Calitri

As part and parcel of any respectable *Calitrani* home, you would expect to find a wine press. We weren't disappointed and soon found one in a recess all to itself. It was of classic design. It featured an internal press with a large wooden screw sporting holes at its top. A nearby long pole was apparently inserted in these holes to rotate the workings and thereby induce enough pressure on the grapes to begin the annual excitement of winemaking.

Our tour complete, we were surprised at how we eventually exited these underground chambers. Judging by our lengthy descent, I had fully expected to have to climb a torturous assent back to the surface. But this was not the case. There, adjacent to the niche, which enclosed the wine press, was a double set of doors. Much to our amazement, they opened onto a *vicolo* leading onto *Via Concezione*, three streets below our entry on *Via Tozzoli*. In our descent, we had, in Pythagorean perfection projected ourselves not only down into the mountainside but also far enough outward, evidenced from the lengthy extent of the grottos, to eclipse multiple streets above and emerge on yet another street. How else could animals have gotten in and out? We resurfaced into the early morning air surprisingly close to Fulvio Moscaritolo's art studio. Clearly this will one day soon become quite the spot in town, transformed undoubtedly by a little cheese, cured ham, some local wine and splendidly appealing artwork.

If, as is said, "life is a restaurant", then Calitri is a cultural buffet. You can pick and choose as you like, when you like, what you like. Stendhal said it best once and I paraphrase very loosely when I say, "There is a joy to being in Calitri, in total freedom without once thinking of the duty to see something." Relax, have some cheese, some *prosciutto*, and, in the vapors of each glass of wine, think not only of *Bacchus* but also of what you'll leave behind someday for others to one day discover.

April, 2008

14

Together Apart

We must have made quite a spectacle that day standing there by the side of that country road outside of Calitri. We were a ragtag bunch for sure in our old clothes, leaning up against the hood of that car, sipping wine in celebration, floppy hats and all. You'd have had to have been there.

Our boots and old shoes were covered in mud. We were tired and dirty from a morning of picking grapes but there was also something just a little different at that moment from when, hours earlier, our morning had begun. It wasn't to be found in how we looked or where we were but in how we now felt. We, all of us, now shared the common expression of broad smiles over what we had accomplished that day, together. For us, it was novelty and more, but for them, it was their way of life, their culture and much more; something we yearned to share in.

Our companions, a local family who had invited us to participate in the harvest, composed of a mother, son, aunt and cousin, was a cut across the dimension of a typical Italian family. Back at home, holding things down until our return,

**29. Our ragtag team celebrates
a successful harvest**

were a sister and father. Together with them we felt part of something greater, rather than like the occasional visitor to a little town in the Italian countryside. At that instant, we felt like we were part of a family, *la famiglia*! Of course we really weren't, for we were and remained *stranieri* (foreigners), but at that moment we were treated like family and felt the embrace of being family.

Since we were Calitri homeowners, we wouldn't necessarily be pigeonholed simply as holidaymakers. We were also more than the typical tourist in a hurry to see the sights and then move on. We couldn't be categorized as that either. Yes, we did come and go so maybe part time resident would categorize us best, if we needed to be categorized at all. I'm sure on occasion we already had been categorized or would be soon. Undoubtedly, as we walked about town, an elderly gentleman here, another there, sitting on a bench and layered in sweaters, would deposit us into one of these pocket designations or pronounce us *Tedesco* (German) like a confident pool player might when calling for the "8-ball in the side pocket". The townspeople require order around them, plausible explanation of any mystery or new face. In all truth, we were gone more than we were there, but still, with time and with more frequent and longer visits, we hoped to be more than observers of cultural phenomenon. We wanted to grab hold of the culture ourselves and actually set up a home in Calitri with the inhabitants. Yes, there would be barriers, many not even visible. We expected that, but we hopefully could accommodate the restrictions, the forlorn bland stares, possibly even a dose of stratified social isolation. Here, at least, we had a beachhead. On that day, we did not feel alone in Calitri, but part of family.

It's not government, not even history, that preoccupies Italians. It is *famiglia*—the single most powerful institution in all of Italy, especially so in the south. It is this essential element that is at the center of Italian culture. While governments, with their shifting rules and regulations, come and go frequently, while inefficiency, corruption, and erratic justice may render them cynical, it is family that can be counted on to last and provide comforting support. Their allegiance is to *famiglia* rather than nation. Family comes before any sense of civic duty, job related or not. It is their first and last loyalty, the center of their being, for family puts order into the everyday disorder and the complicated bureaucracy that is Italy.

La famiglia is the bulwark against all the exigencies of the world outside. Just as bells clanging in a high *campanile* clear the air of all other vibrations and dominate the moment, so the

Italian family is its own refreshing steadfast distraction from reality. If you have family you are never alone.

It is not the same where I come from. In the States, individual husbands and wives, family units, are more independent from the greater family. This is probably due to many factors, among them being our more fluid social structure. We tend to scatter all over due to the mobile nature of our jobs and flexible transportation options. Unmarried children will even move off and live in apartments on their own or with a roommate. Tendrils back to the family can become wispy, even non-existent. This, however, is far from common practice in Italy where unmarried adults tend to remain at home with their parents in the refreshing grace of the family.

The Italian family also transcends distance, even time. They are together even when they are apart. Even the seeming finality of death does not separate them from the cocoon of the *famiglia*. A visit to the Calitri cemetery, in fact any Italian cemetery, illustrates the enduring respect shown the departed. Elaborate little *palazzi* (palaces), with family names engraved in stone above the doorways in an attempt to last forever, border narrow, tree-lined streets. A miniature village for the dear departed. Inside perpetual lights illuminate vaulted walls, which house the dead. Sitting in a simple wooden chair, a family visitor bridges the River Styx and visits with loved ones. Indeed, they are together apart. Here, we meet again with that fabrication called time. In this manifestation, however, it is how time, as in future tomorrows, affects the Italian family. Take Baptism and Easter as examples. Together, they are of monumental religious significance in this most traditionally religious country, but beyond that, they also imbue the family with hope of new life and better times tomorrow, whether for the helpless infant at Baptism or the greater family on the much anticipated occasion of Easter.

I would even go so far as to posit the notion that a garden, so important to the Italian family, is part of its basic yearning that hope of a better tomorrow will assuage the vicissitudes of daily life. Gardens become a therapeutic tonic, helping Italians think beyond the present toward a better tomorrow, even beyond tomorrow to the future. It takes time for a garden to develop, to mature into its design; enough time to become the intent of its caretaker. Still more time to blossom into a tomorrow. It takes time for a seed to germinate, extend its filament roots into the soil and yet more time to explode through the surface seeking sunlight, pollination and space. Cycles of rain, more sun and weeding turn it to succulent stature. Little-by-little yesterday's seed becomes tomorrow's garden bounty for the family to share. Time enough even for cobwebs to form among the tomatoes—at least a tomorrow away. This, being something under theirs and God's control, gives them strength, hope, and the willingness to hold on a little longer and not give up under adversity and injustice. It not only sustains their bodies in uncertain times and emboldens their spirit, but in the bounty of the harvest, it gives them something to share with family. For the family a garden represents generosity in good times and hope for better tomorrows.

That day in a small way, we had come closer together,

connected through the common experience of this shared activity in this vineyard garden. Maria Elena and I were starting our lives in a new way, in a new place, with an adopted new family. We wanted to indulge in the Italian theater of being so alive and so animated. Ours is not a second chance at life, just the continuation of the same life in new environs, among new friends, over new tomorrows. It is a chance to begin again, to renew. Yes, it is exciting. Everything is new and untried—the sights, the smells, the language, the people, the customs, the food, the gestures . . . everything. It's also a chance to observe everything, almost as a child does from birth. To share firsthand a meal and wine with a new neighbor, to stumble over a pronunciation, to participate in their Sunday Masses, to stir the fermenting grape mash for an old widow struggling to continue her traditions, to watch a soccer match and cheer along in a bar full of locals, to look into new eyes. It was a baptism and we were awash in new expectations and experiences, this being but one.

In a small way, we now feel part of something truly Italian. On earlier occasions we had bonded over shared meals, visits, wine, stories and funny situations that only made us laugh as together we experienced them, just as we had shared in the grape harvest.

Some people go to Italy and buy a leather handbag. We bought a house, bought into a dream, the spirit of the place and a new phase of our lives. Away from Calitri, we transcend the distance and maintain our family tie through frequent e-mails, occasional gifts and periodic phone calls in anticipation of our return. So we remain together apart and in the interlude take comfort when hearing us referred to as *Zio Paolo* and *Zia Maria Elena*. Dreams are simply undervalued.

May, 2008

15

Long Anticipated But Fleeting Days

As the Air France steward handed us short-stemmed snifters of cognac, I leaned over and commented to Maria Elena, "You don't even get peanuts on United." What a way to begin a vacation! You know how it is, though. A new day dawns and quickly transits the meridian to become a yesterday. There is never relief from time's relentless progression. This seems especially true while on vacation— that time away from the reality of our everyday lives. Cognac? Get real.

We look forward to our vacations for 'sooo' long—that special time we reserve to relax in new and faraway places and do things we wouldn't normally do. We fantasize and imagine how it will be as the days of the calendar melt away in countdown toward its much anticipated arrival. For a fleeting breath of time, our vacations permit us to change the pond we live in, to visit, however briefly, the proverbial grass on the other side of the fence. We attempt to create, within our fiscal means (and sometimes beyond), a heaven on earth.

The truth is that vacations, however fleeting, are easy to take but so hard to hold onto. Days soon flow into a week or so, and then poof, it's over . . . Events soon relegate themselves to fond memories and a few hasty photos or paint-brushed videos. So what of these fond memories? What is a day of vacation like? Can you remember? Needless to say, it is different for each of us. For us, our recent sojourn in Italy serves as an example of this non-habitual existence—of life off the norm, life displaced from the mundane beaten paths we travel in our work-a-day lives.

The relatively unexplored, sun-filled *mezzogiorno* or southern Italy as it is better known, a fusion of undulating rugged countryside and ridge-hugging villages, is our vacation habitat. As if newly discovered by *Condé Nast* and purveyors in international real estate, the *mezzogiorno*, of late, is now a much talked-up region of Italy due to its affordability, pristine beaches and sun, sun, sun. Having recently returned from our adopted Italian mountaintop town, I can offer a glimpse of what our vacation lives are like in the heart of the *mezzogiorno*, just about equidistant between both coasts.

Our Arrival

It had been like coming home. We were familiar with the place and the place was familiar with us. Work on the castle had continued and all along *Corso Matteotti*, the mason's artistry continued to craft beauty from the decay and rubble remaining from a long-past earthquake. We found our *Borgo* street newly paved in river stone, its length now beautifully illuminated with street lamps, their bell shapes suspended on crooks and leading us to our doorway. Our home was as we'd left it on its miniature, dead-end *piazzatella*. The long key slid into the lock and a few turns later opened the door. We were home.

We received a wonderful reception from friends, who presented us with a wine bottle full of homemade *salsa* (spaghetti sauce), a bag of hazelnuts, and a jug of the wine we had helped make during our last visit. That last visit had been during the grape harvest. This time, our visit apparently coincided with the season when every household blended their annual supply of sauce! Basketfuls of plum tomatoes, their burnt orange colored flesh almost waxen, could be seen throughout town being transported to grottos and homes for their annual culinary transubstantiation. The aroma of pasta sauce hung heavy in the air from grotto to grotto. Clearly, things were done in time-ordered fashion, as nature ordained, and now, with a pastoral rhythm, was the time for the alchemy of salsa making.

We were grateful for help with our luggage. Someday we will learn to travel lighter, with a scruffy travel bag or two,

30. Just arrived, Maria Elena waits by our door

but not this trip. Our three suitcases, in addition to a boxed set of lamps and everything else we had accumulated along the way from Rome, were transferred to a middle-aged Fiat. The Fiat took them into the *Borgo* as far as possible before the sidewalls of the street said no farther. From there they were rolled to our door. Thank God for generous friends with narrow cars and suitcases with rollers! It wasn't long before we were smashing handfuls of hazelnuts on a cutting board with my toolbox hammer and sipping that homemade wine in simple celebration of our safe arrival. It was official now, our vacation was underway.

A Typical Day

Somehow, in the middle of the afternoon, we manage to sleep for hours, but I'm getting a little ahead of myself since our days usually began long before this leisurely afternoon siesta.

Getting up early, ingrained in me through the years, is a part of my fiber . . . and so it goes in Calitri. I'd awaken before 6:00 in the morning to the initial, almost-sounds of a rooster far below us, down the mountainside. His song, not to be denied, wafted in through the long white curtains of our tall balcony doors. At times, he might even be out-shouted by the competing chorus of a pack of discontented dogs off somewhere in the distance. Either way, serenity askew, I was awakened by these heralds of the day and soon on my feet. I'd futz about for a few minutes, trying not to make any noise, long enough for the wall-mounted water heater to gin-up a sufficient supply of hot water. Showered and now dressed, I'd quietly exit *Casa della Feritoia*, while Maria Elena continued her dreamy serenity, hopefully undisturbed by either me or our boisterous farmyard neighbors.

I consider this the best time of the day, before the village actually awakens and the bustle and scurry of daily activity take hold. *Via Berrilli*, just a few steps from our door, is cool and still at this time. It winds me through the *Borgo* to the tunnel through the town hall to deposit me in *Piazza della Repubblica*.

Even by then, a handful of people have gathered by the town hall's doors located in the *piazza*. Town workers and early-bird town-hall patrons chat as Mario sweeps the area in front of his cafe. I sometimes help him set up the green plastic chairs just outside his storefront, symbolic of his arrival, in anticipation of business. The chairs are beacons to early regulars . . .

- Tony Caruso: Mario's verbal sparring partner. Tony was usually in a playful mood despite a painful leg, which kept him awake at night. He and Mario would go round and round each morning in linguistic duals, most of which I couldn't appreciate since they were, most definitely, in Italian, dosed with dialect. These friendly jousts were frequent and included others who would arrive, join in, only to depart after downing their shots of *caffè*. It was interesting how voices would rise as if there was an argument underway, only to melt into laughter. I could never really tell who got the upper hand in their banter.

- Rosina: who you never really get to know as much as you remember and who could be a real-life stand-in for an elderly Laura Ingalls of *Little House on the Prairie* fame. In stoic countenance, she would quietly sit in vigil over the *piazza* from her green plastic throne. In my mind's eye, I can see her sitting there now.

- *Ragazza* Joséphine: the jovial and effervescent owner of the nearby *Centro Market alimentari* (grocery store)

31. Joséphine's Market sign, Calitri

where she can trigger laughter in the specter of a burlesque and where a friendly *grazie* comes bagged with your purchases.

- The mysterious man with no forthcoming name, with a five o'clock shadow and bulging fanny pack slung crosswise across his shoulder in bandolier fashion.

The day at Mario's was developing just as the petals of a flower open each morning to entice the bees. People gather, come to sip their espresso nectar or to just be seen, chatter about events and then disappear in the morning cavalcade of customers.

By 8 a.m., I'd take leave of Mario's to head back to the *casa* and see how Maria Elena was getting along. By then it was time to head downtown for some essentials and for this we'd tote along our two-wheeled shopping cart behind us. From our home in the *Borgo*, it is a short walk into town where we make our rounds, all the while observing around us Calitri and our fellow man . . .

- The morning sun cast lively shadows on nearby walls of the festive ornaments decorating the streets for an upcoming religious celebration.
- Little by little chairs and tables began to appear outside storefronts.
- Men congregate to drink their espressos and read the *La Repubblica* newspaper by each cafe.
- The sun, rising higher in the morning sky, illuminates the wisps of beige-colored dust deposited on the windshields of parked automobiles by African Sirocco winds.
- Through mosquito door-nets, women appear to sweep their door-fronts or shake out a towel, occasionally a rug.
- A Carabinieri patrol passes, on its rounds up to the *piazza* and back down again.
- Men, much like myself, dominate the streets and

32. Carabinieri patrolling Calitri

follow the sun's shadows to cool themselves.

- At Joséphine's, a delivery truck unloads lanky skinned rabbits thoroughly stamped with official inspection seals.

- Poldo's Bar bustles with early activity—*Peroni* beers are already visible outside in the tree shaded sitting area, so reminiscent of a Parisian outdoor cafe.

- Cars begin to double-park, park on curbs or opposite the flow of traffic (we are in Italy after all, not Paris).

- In Zabatta's *pasticceria* (pastry shop), elbow-to-elbow customers jockey for pole position to point out their choice of pastry, biscotti and creamy delicacies.

- But for the DiMiao bus service, there isn't a tourist bus in sight.

It was clear that life had once again taken up residence in Calitri—the town was alive. By 1 p.m., our cart nearly filled, favorites visited, and *buongiornos* liberally sprinkled about, we would return home during that break in the day known as the *riposo*, to eat and rest.

On past visits, Maria Elena had gone out to purchase the things she thought we'd need for our place. I now appreciated what a wonderful job she'd done on her sorties. In fact, we were using our oven for the first time, along with some of the pans and utensils from those shopping sprees, to fashion a delicious meal.

This trip, we'd thought enough ahead to bring along an oven thermometer to help regulate the temperature of our gas oven. I could get it to hold 350 degrees Fahrenheit, about its lowest possible setting and just a smidgen above 'off' on the dial. I'd learned that 350 degrees was that magic number for just about everything baked in an oven. And what a wonderful meal Maria prepared.

We had gone to Anna Maria's *Polleria* (poultry shop) earlier to purchase a freshly roasted chicken. We'd learned that even though it was a chicken store, they only roasted the birds on Thursdays and Saturdays. We had arrived early that Thursday morning to insure we'd be able to snatch one off the rotisserie, only to

33. Market day olive selection, Calitri

realize you had to give them some time to actually roast them. Seems 11:30 a.m. was the magic hour to get one. *Un pollo per Poalo* (a chicken for Paul) became Anna's mantra. But let me get to describing the meal itself and the need for the oven. We had also gone to the *mercato*.

Weekly, on Thursdays, beginning at 9:00 a.m., one of the town's streets is transformed into a combination supermarket, clothing outlet and bric-a-brac. That day our objectives had been hard cheese, olives (enough for the week), colorful plastic tablecloths, *ricotta* and *melanzana* (eggplant).

For lunch, Mare thinly sliced our newly purchased eggplant, dipped it first into an egg batter, then *farina* (flour) and layered it along with local Di Cecca *ricotta fresca* cheese, mixed with ground pepper and garlic, in a baking pan. She then judiciously added some of the equally fresh salsa we'd received as a gift and topped off her creation with grated *parmigiano* cheese. All that was needed was the oven elixir of 350 degrees! I only know one word to describe the outcome—a m b r o s i a .

34. Oven-ready melanzana-ricotta dish

Roasted chicken, the baked *melanzana* ricotta, the *vino* we'd help make and then, to make it obscene, a rum-soaked *dolce* concoction of cloud-light cream and cake completed the meal. In the movie, *The Big Night*, Primo says: "To eat good food is to be close to God." Well, welcome to heaven thanks to the hellish heat of our new oven.

It wasn't long, therefore, before we, like many of the townsfolk, were napping after lunch during the *riposa*. Undoubtedly, the larger lunches accompanied with wine, something we weren't yet accustomed too, helped. We were getting into the rhythm of the place and its lifestyle was getting into us.

By 7 p.m., we'd emerge once again to enjoy the coolness of the evening air and partake in the social poetry of the *passeggiata*, that nightly ritual of strolling where townspeople flood the streets. Part of our evening ritual was to also have a late night slice of pizza or a few warm *arancini* rice balls available from various pizza shops. Of course, the remains of the day wouldn't be complete without *gelato*. A *due gusti* (two scoop) cone of the tangiest and creamiest gelato, only to be found at *Bar Jolly*, was just what the sandman ordered at end of day.

No place is ever only one thing or ever totally understood. Calitri is many things and more than a place. In one instance, it is an inside-out world of courtyards and narrow passageways topped by a castle. What goes on below, in the shadow the castle, however, is what makes up a wonderful life in this little corner of the world. It is a place to come to and take something away from. But not to worry, they have plenty to give! That day the tie that bound us to Calitri had grown a knot stronger. Things were changing and so were we.

Our day complete, the light of day gone to shadow and replaced by a slice of moon, we fell asleep to the soothing sounds of an accordion and the uncontained longing voice of a crooner seated outside the Church of *Santa Lucia*, only to awaken to the reveille of our persistent rooster and go through the experience again. More than a picture, more than a vacation memory poised to fade, that day, we had taken away a little part of Calitri and it was now part of us.

104

October, 2008

Part II
Adventures Farther Afield

**35. Maria Elena with the town square boys,
Sant'Agata dei Goti**

Introduction

Not all of our stories center on Calitri. There are times that we feel an urge to explore nearby areas on day trips about the countryside or to attend festivals in other towns. Sometimes we feel the need to head out from Calitri to experience new, more distant haunts much farther afield.

We are perfectly positioned in the south of Italy, halfway between coasts. The world-renowned Amalfitana Peninsula and Neapolitan coastline lie a little over an hour away, making attractions like Pompeii, Capri, and Sorrento within easy reach. Closer to home, ridge-hugging hilltop communities making up our neighborhood, the Irpinia region of Campania, pepper mountaintops like poppy seeds on a roll. Each warranted a visit.

At other times, while coming to or returning home from Calitri, we make it a point to explore other parts of *Italia*. A high-speed train ride from Naples or bus service from Calitri puts Rome, Venice, Milan, and Lake Como within reach. In our early Italian years, Rome was and still remains a powerful attractant, offering much to see and savor. Farther north, the area of my ancestral homeland, Lake Como, with its enchanting garden estates and convenient ferry shuttle-service to shore-bound picturesque towns, always beckoned.

All this affords a wealth of opportunity to satisfy the growing yearning in Maria Elena and myself to explore beyond the view from our perch high atop Calitri's Borgo and experience other aspects of the grand spectacle that constitutes Italy.

In this section, we relate impressions and memories of some of these more distant parts of the "boot", from head to heel.

16

Certaldo Alto

In our ramblings through Tuscany, we once stayed at an agritourism wine farm just outside of San Gimignano. Off in the distance, we could see the famous towers of San Gimignano, which distinguish this ancient town from all the others in Tuscany. We were actually staying in the town of Ulignano. You would be correct to imagine it as one of those places where if you happened to blink, you'd miss it. Heading away from San Gimignano, to the north, lies the city of Certaldo. No towers here. It is a far more modern city and serves the entire area with a rail link to the rest of Italy.

Within walking distance from the railroad station is a funicular that will take you up to the old, upper city, Certaldo Alto. This charming, medieval walled city is the origin of modern Certaldo, and in typical fashion, is high up on a mountaintop in a defensive position from attack. It is a different world there high above the *Val d'Elsa.* Similar to San Gimignano, but without all the tourists, it features a long main street, *Via Boccaccio.* Still further evidence of its difference is the extensive medieval fortress, *Il Palazzo Pretorio,* located at the upper end of *Via Boccaccio.* Its outside walls are covered with the heraldic coats of arms of the various governors, each appointed by nearby Florence, who occupied the castle following the rule of the Alberti family. The men's and women's dungeons in the bottom reaches of the *palazzo* are especially interesting places to visit. We could only imagine what it must have been like to have been a guest there in its confined spaces.

In addition to the palace, we best recall the upper city for the bust of the god of wine, Bacchus, we purchased while there. It now hangs in our stateside kitchen, not far from a drawer-bound corkscrew. Our other memory is of the small, family-run sandwich shop we discovered located on the left side of *Via Boccaccio*, about three-quarters of the way to the palace and just past an old well. It's easy to find.

We've been there twice now. The first time was all discovery, while the second time was to reminisce. Even in the span of only the few years that separated our visits, things had already changed—the sandwich shop in particular. When first we visited, it was mostly a small market for residents with aisles of packaged and canned goods and a deli, demarcated from the rest of the establishment by a glass-faced cooler at the far end. Some of the cans, like the olive cans and the cans of marinated artichokes, were open, beckoning a passerby to reach in. It is not a large place by any means. There was only enough room for a few aisles in addition to shelves adorning the sidewalls.

Upon our return, we found it had become mostly a sandwich place and less of a market. It was also apparent that the proprietors had changed, which may account for the change in business emphasis. A mother and her son now oversaw the operation. A *mezzo* liter of the house red and a custom-made roast pork and provolone sandwich was absolutely satisfying. Patrons can select everything they want in your sandwich right down to the thickness of the crusty Italian bread they'll slice for you. And don't forget to include one (or two) of those olive oil soaked artichokes to go along with whatever else you may order, we didn't.

December, 2006

36. Enjoying lunch in Certaldo

17

Hollywood on Lake Como

Have you seen the James Bond movie, *Casino Royale,* where 007 is recuperating (yes, he actually bleeds now!)? Or perhaps the *Star Wars: Episode I – Attack of the Clones* scene where young Jedi Anakin marries beautiful Padme Amidala? The settings for these scenes were one and the same, not the stuff of a Hollywood back lot or green screen technology. Both were filmed on dazzling Lake Como, not far from Milan. An interesting aside is that the holy-man, who married young Darth Vader and the Naboo senator, is a local Lake Como dentist.

37. Villa Balbianello, Lake Como

The actual site is *Villa del Balbianello*, very near the little lakeside town of Lenno. It is located on the tip of the Lavedo peninsula, a small, wooded promontory jutting from the western shore of Lake Como, not far from the island of Isola Comacina. The villa is famous for its enchanting, elaborate terraced gardens. They are not expansive by any means, but they are unlike any we've seen before. This place is simply enchanting, almost mystical.

The grand villa was built in 1787 for Cardinal Angelo Maria Durini. Overlooking the bays of Diana and Venus, it now belongs to FAI (*Fondo per l'Ambiente Italiano*), a national trust for public education regarding environmental protection and the conservation of Italy's artistic and monumental heritage. They certainly have one here. By the way, the story goes that the cardinal had a coffin in his bedroom along with his bed to remind him of his mortality and final disposition. It must have, for he was buried in it.

Villa Balbianello and its wonderful gardens are open to the public from April to October. A guide, especially useful for those behind the scene stories, must accompany visitors wishing to explore the villa's interior rooms. The one we met was present at the *Villa Balbianello* location shoot for the Star Wars Episode. She had a wealth of stories about the filming, and about Hayden Christensen, Natalie Portman and George Lucas—not gossipy, just neat little details about the site, the people, and how pleased the locals were with how beautiful Lake Como was presented, and how the film crew was warm and polite their entire stay. Also filmed there was *A Month by the Lake*, the 1995 film with Vanessa Redgrave.

The villa can be reached by private shuttle boat service from Sala Comacina, a little village just up the coast from Lenno, or by foot from Lenno itself (about a half mile trek out along the ridge of the peninsula). We particularly enjoyed this walk through the forest canopy and the views into interesting lakeside backyards.

January, 2007

18

In the Hands of God

I was thinking back to an earlier trip to Italy, back in 2000 in fact. It was our second adventure to *Bella Italia*. We landed in Milan and spent time in the area around Lake Como. One day, we decided to make a daytrip farther west to see what Lake Maggiore and Lago d'Orta were all about.

Maggiore (also called Verbano) is 55 km (34 miles) from Milan's Malpensa Airport but otherwise a world away. Without question, Lake Maggiore is far less glitzy than Como, less crowded than Lake Garda, and overall a more natural experience. Lake Maggiore is Italy's second biggest lake. It acts

38. Santa Caterina Hermitage, Lake Maggiore

as a watery boundary between two Italian regions, Lombardy and Piedmont, with its northern tip extending into Switzerland.

Isola Bella is an island in Lake Maggiore. It is here that you will find *Palazzo Borromeo*, an Italian baroque palace, as well as terraced Italian gardens, giving it the appearance of an enormous tiered wedding cake. They even refer to it as the Wedding Cake Island. Though one of the big tourist draws on Lake Maggiore, and indeed beautiful, we never got there. Instead, we opted for a short ferry trip from the Stresa boat launch across the lake to its cliff-lined eastern shore. Here we found the *Hermitage Santa Caterina del Sasso*, which conveyed a very different emotion from Isola Bella; a triumph of man, to this, a rejoicing in God. To us it presented a more spiritual, almost mystical setting. We were taken by its sense of simple holiness—far different from the grander and opulence of better-known attractions such as *St. Mark's Basilica*.

This historic sanctuary has clung to the rocky cliffs of Sasso Ballaro since the 12th century. It is an incredible feat of engineering and religious devotion. Its beginning stems from the day when a wealthy merchant and moneylender named Alberto Besozzi was sailing on the lake. The furor of a sudden storm capsized his boat.

"He prayed to Saint Catherine of Alessandria to save him, which she seemingly did — an enormous wave swept Alberto up and deposited him on a rocky ledge below the cliffs. In gratitude, he dedicated the next forty years of his life to Saint Catherine — spending every

day of those forty years in a cave as a hermit. Locals lowered food and water to him in a basket."[1]

During this time, Alberto developed quite a reputation for his piety, and soon attracted others to his cause. Surprisingly, we were able to see him the day we visited because his mortal remains are encased in a glass sarcophagus to the rear of the main altar room. Adding to this experience was the heavenly sound of unseen monks somewhere behind vaulted doors. Their voices in angelic Gregorian chant were transportive, only adding to the religious intimacy.

39. Piazza in Orta San Giulio, Lake Orta

Still in the glow of spiritual enlightenment upon returning to our departure point in Stresa, we were immediately reoriented back to earthly matters with the discovery of a bureaucratic gift to humanity—a parking ticket. It seems I'd parked our little Fiat Bravo between the wrong colored lines.

---

1   Lake Maggiore: Fanciful and Fantastic - GoNomad Travel, www.gonomad.com

Here is a tip: In Italy, white lines indicate free public spaces while blue lines are pay-to-use public spaces. Look for a parking ticket dispenser somewhere in the area, pay the fee, and then display the receipt on your dashboard. It will save you at least 60,600L (about $32). Oh, the high cost of education. Angry, then frustrated, my immediate reaction was to refuse to pay the fine. We drove away. After all, I asked myself, how would they ever catch up with us—tourists from half a globe away in a rental?

Our next destination was adjacent Lake Orta. Only 8 miles long by 2 miles wide, Lago d'Orta is one of the smallest of the Italian Lakes. It's also a lake few tourists seem to know. Many locals wish it would remain that way. Beginning at the top of the lake, we skirted its eastern shore until we reached Orta San Giulio. This exquisite little town is nicknamed "soul of the lake." No cars are allowed in this shore-side gem. After carefully parking on the outskirts (this time paying close attention to the colored lines and elusive ticket dispenser boxes), we walked into town and soon arrived at an intersection with *Via Bossi*, apparently the town's main thoroughfare. On October 31, 2005, *Italy Magazine* wrote . . .

"Via Bossi, a narrow Medieval street lined with tiny shops leads you past the terracotta-coloured 'municipio', where summer weddings take place in the garden overlooking the lake, to Piazza Motta, the town's central square. Like the best box in the most prestigious of theatres, the piazza is positioned so all seats command a view of the Isola di San Giulio, the

most beautiful of all the lakes' islands. At the far end of the piazza is the once-grand Albergo d'Orta, on the left tiny shops and bars below a row of 17th century houses painted in shades of yellow, the palest pinks and blues."

It was here that we found and entered an apparently minor, simple faced stone church. Its plain interior and the heavy scent of wax bespoke its years of service to the townspeople. Upon exiting, we noted an apartment overlooking the street with a *vendesi* (for sale) sign in its window. In another apartment, just above it, a small yellow sign was inscribed, Padre Pio. A passerby, who happened to be a postal official, informed us that the sign was in response to an apparition attributed to Padre Pio. Padre Pio, it seems, had appeared up where we could see the sign. At street level, below this miraculous apartment, a small shop selling religious items conveniently displayed pictures of Padre Pio.

Leaving Padre Pio's country behind, we continued toward *Piazza Motta.* We soon happened upon a *salumeria* (a shop specializing in salami) where the proprietor, hearing us talking over what to order, began to talk to us in English. In addition to our lunch order, I got around to mentioning our Stresa parking experience. By this time, I was having misgivings. I imagined an Interpol all-points bulletin, threatening letters from Hertz when we returned home, or customs officers pulling us into an interrogation room (suspended ceiling lamp and all) on some future return to Italy.

He advised us to pay the fine. If we had rented in France or Germany and driven into Italy we may have been OK, but . . .

We also gained another interesting dollop of knowledge: you can pay a fine at just about any post office. It didn't have to be in Stresa where my civil infraction occurred. These Italians, at least concerning money, were organized! About then, I wondered if the collecting commune also got a taste of the payment in return.

It wasn't long after our lunch under the chestnut trees of the piazza that we were on the road south to Borgonmanero and its post office. It was the closest one still open this time of day. Unfortunately, we had no specific directions on how to get there. When we eventually arrived, we'd be on our own when it came to finding the post office. I'd thought it would be a small town but was I wrong. At a traffic light, a motorcycle had pulled up beside us. Fortunately for us, he'd obeyed the traffic light and stopped, unlike what many of his compatriots would have done. I rolled down the window and asked the man where it was. To my *"Dove è l'ufficio postale?"* (Where is the post office) inquiry, his rapid reply was unintelligible.

Though I'd listened to enough CDs to know how to ask this, my comprehension of his reply was still weak. He realized this and motioned that we should follow him. Off our guardian angel went, snaking through town with us trailing close behind. Minutes later, he motioned toward a building, waved, and was off again before I could attempt a proper thank you. We would have looked a long time for the place without the appearance of our Good Samaritan.

I got in line and queued-up with a group of women. Not one to keep quiet for long, I started a conversation trying to relate my parking ticket plight. At one point I put my arms out to mimic being handcuffed and when they couldn't understand me I said, *"Come OJ,"* (meaning like O.J. Simpson) which had gone viral in the news. That they understood

40. Paolo pays his parking fine, Borgonmanero

and they all proceeded to laugh. What were they doing there? Well, certainly not buying postage stamps or paying parking violations. It seems that in Italy, financial transactions occur at the post office. All sorts of bills are paid there and that's what they were patiently, patiently waiting to do.

The hermit placing himself in God's hands, the miraculous apartment apparition of Padre Pio, the postman, leading to the San Giulio shopkeeper's counsel to pay the parking ticket, and later the sudden appearance of that angel mounted on a motorcycle helping us find our way to the post office—What can I say? The Fates in control of our lives? The guiding hand of God? All coincidence? I can't decide.

January, 2007

41. Maria Elena on commuter train, Rome

Realpolitik: *politics based on practical objectives rather than on ideals; a politics of adaptation to things as they are.*

19

Railroad Politique

Years ago, after our arrival for the first time in Rome, we had quite an experience with what I call the train police. At our bed and breakfast north of Rome, our hosts gave us rail passes and instructed us to stamp them, using the yellow boxes on the train, immediately upon boarding. We were novices without question, as I said, first timers. From the station at Grottarossa, we followed their instructions and enjoyed our first foray into the Eternal City, that first afternoon of our arrival. We understood that the tickets were good for *24 ora.* Since we had activated them around 2:00 p.m. that day, we believed they would be valid until 2:00 p.m. the next day. We would then purchase new all-day rail passes. That was the plan, but boy were we wrong.

The next morning, again seated on the train headed back to Rome's *Piazza del Popolo*, the ticket inspector asked for our tickets. I produced mine and upon inspection was immediately told it was no good. It was expired! In the half-English, half-Italian exchange that followed (actually on my part it was more English than Italian), I tried to explain that the *biglietto* (ticket) was good for *24 ora* beginning at 2:00 p.m. *ieri* (yesterday). Unfortunately, this was not the case. Good for 24 hours of a day, it did not extend past midnight. I needed to pay a mega fine on the spot and since there were, in fact, two of us, it was *doppio* (double)!

Since it was an early morning train into the city, there were a number of fellow ticket checkers on board. They were apparently on their way to work—headed into Rome from the suburbs to deploy throughout the municipal system. They all looked like they'd just won the PGA Masters Championship due to their identical green sports jackets with shiny buttons. Now that I knew what they looked like, I persisted in my argument.

The ticket cop would go back and forth from me to his grouped colleagues for apparent consultation. After a few round trips, I could tell that by dribs and drabs, I was losing this argument. Although I had first appealed to being an uninformed tourist, then to misinformation, and in a final attempt to make my case that they could easily give me a break, they were almost to a man in favor of the double fine. I could just imagine one of them in the huddle saying, "These tourists always claim ignorance."

One official, however, was sympathetic to our plight and favored letting us go with a warning just as a traffic cop does on occasion in the States. Finally out of arguments, I said I do not lie, cheat, or steal. It was not how I operate. They probably couldn't comprehend such a statement. Culturally, I believe Italians play a game with authorities, including government agencies of all form, in order to minimize higher authority's effectiveness as it attempts to control their lives. A classic example is the energy they expend and the pleasure they take in avoiding taxes. That being said, and I don't know why I thought to do it, but from my wallet I pulled out my military ID and stated that I was a pilot in the U.S. Air Force. This was true but I was actually retired, and mine was a retiree's military ID. Instantly something changed. It was like magic. Only recently did I read the following, which may help explain what happened:

> *"Few decisions are allowed to be influenced by sentiments, tastes, hazards or hopes, but usually by a careful valuation of the relative strength of the contending parties. The choice between one alliance or another, between hostility or peace, resistance to the last breath or immediate surrender, are the result of a realistic estimate of the forces each side can marshal."* [1]

By no means was this an instance of warfare, but there was no question that contending interests were definitely at stake. Authority up against sophomoric ignorance with only two.

When these officials saw what I'd produced, and understood my words, the issue was immediately resolved in my favor. Their hands went up and many *nessun problèma* (no problem) ensued. The sudden appearance of my ID had somehow changed everything.

---

1   Barzini, Luigi. *The Italians*. 1ˢᵗed. New York: Touchstone, 1996. 384. Print.

They may have thought I was attached to the U.S. Embassy in Rome. I can only attribute the sudden turn of events to a shift in relative power. To save face and insure I purchased a valid day ticket, one of them would accompany us to the ticket window upon arrival at the Flaminia Station. Unwilling to tamper with magic, "*Nessun problèma,*" was all I said.

There would be other days, other battles fought with different dialectic shifts and outcomes, but this was the start. If we ever hoped to understand Italy, we had better understand the train ticketing system. That day, though we were in the wrong, I harbored a hidden smile. I'd learned something, not fully understood until years later, about my fellow man.

February, 2007

20

Getting to Calitri —
The Long Way Around

In March of 2007, we were getting ready to once again depart for Italy. This time, we planned to depart the Saturday before Easter. It was early in the year, sure, but this would ensure we were some steps ahead of the annual migration of tourists, although when you think about it, we are tourists ourselves. I can't say that the euro to dollar exchange rate was inviting though. With the rate at 1€ per $1.33, I knew what it must feel like for all those Canadians who come to the States.

42. The Doge Palace, Venice

By nature, I am a maker of lists and a planner. Now that we have a place of our own in Calitri, my lists, like my cup, runneth over. Call me anal retentive if you must, but I have computer lists on the items we need to buy for *Casa della Feritioa,* house matters we need to address while there, lists of area restaurants and wineries to investigate, places to shop for odds and ends, questions I'd like answered, ViaMichelin directions to a number of places in the hope we won't get lost, lists of things to remember to bring with us, even an accounting of the items we will take with us for the apartment, just in case customs asks. Whew, and there are more. Nevertheless, I invariably forget something if I don't make a list. So I start early and keep track of details through lists. That's one of the nice things about traveling; The elixir of anticipation long before you leave.

Armed with my lists, we were planning to depart from Boston, with a plane change in Paris and then on to Marco Polo Airport in Venice, our first sojourn. We were flying Air France. This would be our first trip on AF. Unfortunately, we'd not travel as first-class passengers. No chance to sample the French wines.

One other concern had been about the Charles de Gaulle Airport and its lost baggage reputation. With a three-hour layover, you'd think that would be enough time to move some bags on the same carrier. Fingers crossed, I was hoping for the best.

Now, regarding my apprehensions about Charles de Gaulle airport. We'd heard stories. However, I can report that we thoroughly enjoyed our Air France flight and that the airport was beautiful and efficient. So far, so good with Air France and its Paris hub. I can also report that no bags were lost along the way, which because we had two large bags of household items along with us, was a major concern. They made it all the way through from when we wished them adieu and good luck in Boston.

Using vacuum space bags, we removed the air and really compressed the softer items. This permitted us to fit all the apartment cloth items (towels, sheets, etc) in one suitcase. In another suitcase, we placed metal objects, like utensils for the kitchen. But then I became concerned that if someone scanned the suitcase with the space bag, got curious about something and pulled it for physical inspection, the baggage cops might open one of the vacuum bags. If that happened, and barring a nearby vacuum cleaner, I worried whether things, now expanded, would once again fit in the suitcase. It would make repacking by an inspector impossible. I was asking for trouble but maybe just a little over the top with unnecessary concern. Then again, isn't that the idea behind insurance? To reduce the likelihood of a space bag inspection, we repacked to remove all the metal items from that suitcase. The second suitcase, what we referred to as the apartment suitcase, now contained all the metal items. They could have fun with that one because if scanned, it would show one heck of a metal blob.

I went as far as to include a letter in large font print in each suitcase, which said: *"The items in this bag are for my private use in the apartment I own in Calitri, Italy."* This was in way of explanation in the hope of warding-off any Value Added Tax (VAT) from custom inspectors concerned about resale. I also included my address at home and in Calitri. All told, there were eight rolling suitcases in our traveling group of four. For you older types, when we moved, en masse, it was like the circus had come to town. In this case, an extended train of clicking two-wheeled suitcases. It was especially a sight to behold when our circus played in Venice!

We were going to Venice to show my sister and brother-in-law around. This was their first trip to Italy. We were starting at the top and gradually working our way southward. It would be great adventure—We as would-be guides, my sister and brother-in-law, trusting novitiates. Hopefully much better than the blind leading the blind.

Years earlier, Maria Elena and I enjoyed a day trip to Venice by train. This time, with four days to look forward to, especially

43. Our suitcase burdened group in Venice

after nightfall, we would all get to see it together and breath-in its romantic atmosphere.

We stayed in the Dorsoduro district at the *Palazzo Guardi,* a stone's throw, as they say, from the *Ponte dell'Accademia* (Accademia Bridge). It came highly rated from *Trip Advisor*, and practically anywhere else I checked. It was a former Venetian palace, but then in Venice just about everything is. Our apartment's location was almost a mystery for us to uncover because it was located in an alleyway not much wider than a yardstick. It was an interesting adventure, just to find it. This went well with an Easter egg hunt theme since it was Pasque (Easter) when we arrived. I still recall rolling our suitcases, many of them unfortunately, down that narrow *calle* (a Venetian street). We were fortunate though, because we were given rooms in what they called the Annex. Our view overlooked the small *Rio de San Trovaso* canal, not the ally-way. With a right turn out our doorway, *Rio de San Trovaso* connected to the famous Grand Canal.

If instead we turned left and followed the lane along the canal, it was a short walk and footbridge away to the broad *Giudecca Canal*, lined with outdoor cafes and restaurants. We loved our place—convenient location and great value for the undervalued dollar. As an added treat, downstairs, just below our windows, was a small tavern by the name of *Taverna San Trovaso*. Following a meal there, we highly recommend it.

Our accommodations were definitely off the beaten track from the hectic *San Marco* district, but not for want of interesting places, cafes, piazzas, even a nearby *mercato* to restock on nibbles. Besides, in a walking city like Venice, where even bikes are forbidden, along with skates and skateboards, when we crossed over the Accademia Bridge, we were only ten minutes from St. Mark's.

Getting back to my suitcase theme, you could easily spot us on the *vaporetto* water bus system with our baggage train. From their number, any curious observer might have scratched their head and wondered where we could possibly be headed and for how long! It wasn't until our last day there, when we were leaving on the water taxi for *Ferrovia Santa Lucia* to catch a train, that we saw a sign on the boarding platform wall announcing that travelers were restricted to just one bag each on these boats. Oops, it was too later by then, for rogues that we were, we were on a roll.

Were our precautionary efforts rewarded? It's hard to tell because there was no evidence that our bags were ever searched, even opened. When we retrieved our bags at our first stop in Venice, we just walked through customs. They weren't interested, at least not in us. So maybe my strategy was

44. Our agro-tourism cottage in Chiusi, Tuscany

successful or maybe it was overkill and a waste of time. Will we ever know? Maybe on our next trip with the space bags because we return soon.

After our stay in Venice, we would take the train to Florence and stay a total of two days and a wake-up before moving on. Being centrally located, it would be a short walk to the famous *Piazza della Signoria.* Walking the inner city in the days to follow would be an adventure, new to all of us. On past day-trips to Florence by train, we were limited by time and had specific visit objectives in mind. This time, we could roam and take time to enjoy this city of beauty and art.

After this sojourn, we would say goodbye to the big metropolises and drive south into the heartland of Tuscany. Our first stop would be at IKEA on the outskirts of Florence to see what we could find from our list of things needed for Calitri. Have I mentioned that means just about everything? By then, the van we'd be driving should just about be at spill-over full. Our next planned destination was Chiusi in southern Tuscany, just off the A-1 *Autostrada.* We had a closely held, special place there in the countryside, not far from Lake Trasimino. Two attached and beautifully modern Tuscan cottages awaited us. We would use this as a base camp of sorts to explore farther into Tuscany and Umbria over the next few days.

The next and final leg of our adventure was to Calitri. It was a long drive to get there from Chiusi. I expect the anticipation of walking into our new home for the first time made the trip seem even longer. I considered carrying Maria Elena over the

1875 dated threshold, but only for an instant! Unfortunately, we had to bypass *Roma*, but two out of the big three wasn't bad for first timers. This would be compensated for by the many out-of-the-way, side adventures we experienced. We had fun unpacking all our purchases and setting up the place, something my wife and *sorella* (sister) had been looking forward to. It's surprising how long their excitement at this lasted.

March, 2007

21

Smokey and the Bandit

It was April 2007, and it was as if it were yesterday. We were spending a week in Calitri, getting our bearings and doing all those things to set up our place to our liking (cleaning, painting, shopping for household item, hanging curtains, more painting).

Sometimes when we ventured out and were driving toward Avellino, for instance, for a little shopping at Progress (a combination IKEA, Target, and Sears store) or to Pompeii, we were stopped by the police. This didn't happen once but three

45. Typical carabinieri patrol car, Lucca

times during that two week trip. Boy, they must have been watching me closely because from all their stops, they sure knew my whereabouts and travel pattern to a T. I'm surprised that by the third stop they didn't ask, *"Come siete oggi, Paolo?"* (How are you today, Paul?)

Since then I've learned a little bit more about Italian police forces. Italian public security is provided by five separate police forces:

Arma dei Carabinieri - Military Police.

Guardia di Finanza - Financial and Customs police, also organized as a military force.

Polizia di Stato - State Police.

Polizia Penitenziaria - Penitentiary Police.

Corpo Forestale dello Stato - Forestry Police.

Additionally, some provinces also operate a local form of police called *Polizia Provinciale* (Provincial Police) and all city councils have their local *Polizia Municipale* (Municipal Police), although their responsibilities are mostly of traffic control and enforcement of local city or regional laws.[1]

These repeated stops had nothing to do with traffic violations but seemed to be some sort of random checks. As for the randomness of it, I hadn't been winning at this game.

---

1   A compilation from "Law Enforcement in Italy" <http:// en.wikipedia.org>

Contrary to what you may think, or may be used to back home, there doesn't seem to be a need for cause to stop you in Italy. You know, a headlight out, weaving, an expired inspection sticker, etc.—some sort of violation to justify pulling you over.

Highway SS7 is a main east-west road in our area. But for the *Autostrada* farther north, this winding, though colorful, state road is a major artery of transit. The absence of a toll probably also influences its traffic volume. I suspect the *Carabinieri* were looking for run-of-the-mill reprobates, what my British friends call hooligans, and other nasty characters such as drug traffickers, possibly smugglers, or maybe even your occasional car thief. How about a rascal American or two?

As I'd come around a corner, an officer with a long handled paddle in his hand, topped by a disk with a large "X" placard on its face, would wave us over and ask for my papers. These were *Carabinieri* officers. I would produce my American driver's license, international driver's license, rental-car documents, and threw in my retired military ID for good measure. Only at one of these stops was I asked for my passport. I usually carry a photocopy with me but, unfortunately, not that day. The officer told me I should carry it with me at all times. My thought at the moment were an amusement best kept to myself. In the Campania countryside? In the middle of nowhere? I explained that it was back in our home in Calitri. Apologizing profusely for my lapse, I wholeheartedly agreed and assured him I would carry it with me faithfully on every future outing. Think of this as major groveling on my part!

Each time they would go back to their vehicles—those neat ones with *"Carabinieri"* all along the sides and roofs festooned with lights and sirens—and fill out more forms (Italian bureaucrats certainly love their paperwork and large ledgers). And me, thinking I'd be off the grid leaving my cell phone and computer behind while on vacation. Who was I kidding? By the third stop, they had me pinpointed better than a GPS fix.

A little intimidating, they sported bulletproof vests and machine guns. No, I'm not kidding. This helps explain why I am so humble in their presence. Be assured, they are not to be toyed with and as with all police, they can't help but be intimidating in their voice, mannerisms and appearance. They honestly have to be trained in this as a technique. It's hard to even get a smile out of them. With those spiffy uniforms with a crimson strip down their pant leg, bleach white sashes, epilates, high jack-boots, and caps adorned with a golden flaming insignia, they would merit the envy of any of our state police.

When back in Calitri, I asked some locals what this was all about and all anyone seemed to say was *controlo* (control). If you visit, be prepared for some of your own *controlo* encounters. And, oh, if stopped on SS7, be sure to give them my regards and humbly inform them, *Paolo dice ciao* (Paul says hello)!

June, 2007

46. Friendly pair of police officers, Florence

47. The Temple of Ceres, Paestum

22

Ubiquitous Stone

The sun had not yet risen when Lucius heard the sounds. They were pulling him back from his dreams. Dogs barked. Their bark heralded the approach of something. Perhaps riders from Agropolis or possibly farmers arriving with their produces for market day accounted for the commotion. Today was market day after all, wasn't it? There was something else. Ah, the breeze was up and the canvas over mama's stall fluttered with a dull popping sound. Sleep was retreating.

Though his mother had often scolded him for leaving the house this early, especially by himself, Lucius nevertheless jumped from his bed, threw water on his face from the nearby cistern and stealthily headed for the street, just outside, to investigate. He'd take his chances that his mother wouldn't catch him or that some city vagrant wouldn't bother with him, regardless of what momma had warned.

Outside now, looking west toward the Porta Marina city gate, Lucius could just make out the outlines of lumbering animals approaching. As they came closer, he began to make out the shapes of wagons coming into view through the early morning fog and the smoke from countless home-fires. More sounds, this time from the wagon wheels, added to the cacophony as they made their continuous grinding rounds over the uneven, dark stone pavement. The sound of dogs yelping at the laboring draft *animals served to amplify it further. The city was awakening, roused just as he had from slumber. The caravan of ox-drawn wagons groaned and creaked from their loads as they slowly made their way by the low stone structure he comfortingly called home. He stood under the canvas awning and watched the advancing file. Interspersed here and there in the long train where gruesome looking ex-legionnaires guarding the shipment from their chariots. Their gladius short-swords at the ready made the silent statement - do not come closer.*

As they passed by, Lucius noticed grain, a little here, a little there, slipping through gaps in the wagon's sideboards, added to every so often by an especially violent jostle from the rocky roadway. Apparently the dockworkers had worked through the night to unload the long awaited grain ships from Sicilia. They turned by the Forum and headed down the Cardo Maximus deeper into the city toward the temples of Apollo and Juno where priests would offer sacrifice in thanksgiving for this bounty. As he focused on the escaping granules, he smiled inwardly. Momma would be pleased with him when, after gathering it up, he'd present it to her. As the city began to stir, his dream now was of the freshly baked bread he would enjoy this day. It was auspicious. The gods and momma would indeed be merciful today.

What would my imagined scene in ancient Paestum, just south of Salerno and the Amalfi Coast, really have been like on that day in 200 BC? Vibrant and alive with the activity of thousands of people, this once important coastal city was destined to be abandoned, forgotten, and eventually lost in time, not to be rediscovered until the 18th century.

Let's begin with a brief look at Paestum's history and finish with what we found when we visited in 2007 after driving over from Calitri. For the historical synopsis which follows, I drew from far more learned minds, paraphrased from various Internet sources to piece together the early story of Paestum.[1]

History has relatively little to report concerning the settlement of Paestum. We first knew of it as Poseidonia, a name originally bestowed in honor of the god of the sea, Poseidon. We also know that it was first colonized by Greeks from Sybaris, the mother city of Poseidonia, around 600 BC. Sybaris was a prosperous city in its own right, positioned on the Ionian Sea, located in today's Italian province of Calabria, south of Paestum.

The entire area, extending from Paestum surprisingly as far south to include Sicily, was known as *Magna Grecia* or Greater Greece. This term denoted the expansive Greek colonization into Italy, which began around 800 BC. Poseidonia was located south of the Sele River. Interestingly, in 1943, this was the American section of beach in the invasion of mainland Italy during WWII. As it had been the dividing line between British and American forces, it was this river that had formed a natural boundary between Greek (southern) and Etruscan (northern) domination on the peninsula. Unfortunately, the sacking of the mother city Sybaris, in 510 BC, sparked the hasty migration of many Greeks in search of safety, northward to Poseidonia.

---

1   Much of the historical information about Paestum was derived from: <http://sights.seindal.dk/sight/86_Paestum.html> and <http://www.localidautore.com/primopiano/regione/campania-4/the-archaeological-site-of-paestum-1932.aspx>

Archeologists have linked the apparent rise in city development through construction, which coincided with the influx of these émigrés. As a crossroad of trade routes, Paestum thrived. Fertile soil and an abundance of water assured its success. Around 400 BC, the Lucan tribe, an indigenous Samnite people living farther inland, ended the 200 year Greek rule of the city.

Only conjecture remains concerning the reason for the conquest. It is speculated that the desire for more farmland may have been the driving force behind the invasion. The Lucanians conquered Poseidonia and ruled the area for approximately the next 600 years in a relatively laissez-faire manner. Other than control, little change occurred from the Lucanian conquest. In fact, it retained much of its Greek character. Greek remained the official spoken and written language, religious institutions were maintained, along with continuity in regional trade. Although Poseidonia was lost to the Greek political sphere of influence, it remained Greek in every other sense.

Big changes in Poseidonia came with the arrival of the Romans. Farther to the north, those pesky Romans, having by this time consolidated their domination over the Etruscans through a series of wars, crossed the Sele River in 273 BC and took control of the city. Poseidonia had been on friendly terms with Rome, but during the war (280-275 BC) between Pyrrhus, a relative of Alexander the Great, and Rome, the inhabitants of Poseidonia made the fateful mistake of siding with the losing side. After Pyrrhus' defeat, Rome took revenge on Poseidonia.

Losers in wars often suffer and the Greeks of Poseidonia

were no exception. Much changed, beginning with the population. Latin colonists arrived, took control the city and supplanted the Greeks, many of whom may have been killed or displaced in the process. It was the Romans who also gave the city its Latin name, Paestum, and transformed it into a Roman model in its layout and culture. Compared to the Lucanian period, what followed were major physical changes from its Greek identity. Rome installed its political, social and religious institutions. A common city plan, typical of Roman colonies, was implemented. Two paved roads were introduces, crisscrossing the city through its center, effectively dividing the city into four quadrants. The city space was greatly redeveloped to make room for Roman style administrative and religious buildings. The Forum, which was the political and social center of the city, was positioned near the intersection of the two main roads, completely replacing what the Greeks called a gathering place or agora. Life and death continued.

So what happened severe enough to see the city abandoned? Well, it wasn't a sudden massive volcanic explosion, which buried the city in ash. Instead, we're told, disease and warfare took their gradual tolls. By the time of the late Roman Empire, the population had been decimated. The dual ravages of malaria from nearby coastal marshes and raids from Saracen forces from Agropolis, attempting to expand their power across the Mediterranean as the Greeks had earlier, accounted for its demise. By the 9th century AD the city had undergone serious social decline. The area surrounding the city gradually turned into swampland when calcification problems with the natural springs became unmanageable. Population steadily declined and eventually the infrastructure collapsed. For the inhabitants, it proved easier to live elsewhere, as for instance in the mountains, inland, to the east. By the 12th century, Paestum was completely deserted. Now lost to the world, it was eventually overgrown by forest and not re-discovered until 1752 by a road building crew. Not until 1779, however, was the city actually identified and even then, little excavation occurred. As recently as the end of World War II, allied aerial photographs confirm the area remained relatively untouched since its unearthing. We actually saw archeologists busy excavating when we visited, since much of the city still remains to be rediscovered.

So much for its long history. Looking at it today, it is difficult to imagine that life once flourished across this coastal area of the Cilento. Gone are the malaria-laden mosquitoes, marshlands, and invaders—unless you consider tourists like us, the new interlopers. Laid out before us was the evocative site of a former great city ravaged by centuries of decay. It lay there void of color. Striped of its stature and clearly its former splendor, all that remained in the rust of time was the travertine stone skeleton of a broken city.

Maria Elena and I, arriving at this UNESCO World Heritage site 26 centuries after its founding, felt humbled as we explored the rocky outcroppings and magnificent ancient Greek temples for which Paestum is famous. Though far from the first to survey it, it was fascinating to explore these ruins that harbored a graveyard silence to themselves. In a sense, we felt the excitement of Schliemann when he'd rediscovered Troy.

In places, only the footprints or rough outlines of buildings remain, best seen from the air. It lay there in daydream abandon—not a monument or statue remained. The ruins that are visible today are almost all from the Roman period, with the exception of the three great temples. While most of the walls and pillars were missing, doubtlessly victims of cannibalizing stone vandals through the centuries, you couldn't help but imagine what it had been like in its day, before the lethal effects of neglect. It is nothing like the far more intact cities of Pompeii or Herculaneum farther to the north, but still amazing how you can make out the layout of once opulent homes. The extent of it, the fraction that has been excavated so far, only added to the mystique during our visit.

Through what must have once been doorways, confirmed by the level spaces between now dwarfed stone sidewalls, we walked in a maze-like pattern. It wasn't easy for our untrained eyes to decipher the function each enclosure may have once served. Unlike a traditional maze, however, here there was no fear of becoming disoriented. While all around us were stones, their diminutive stature permitted us to maintain an unrestricted view in any direction – Temple Ceres to the north and the side-by-side Temples of Hera and Neptune to the south. We were Gullivers in a Lilliputian world of stone!

We could make out the peristyle garden areas in the interiors of many homes. Now all that remained were their empty rectangular pools. At one time, they had been surrounded by covered colonnaded walkways. Today, only eroded column stubs remain as evidence. It was easy to imagine the sound of water in the coolness of these garden havens and the rooms, grouped around them, drawing in fresh air from the open roofs above the pools. We were fascinated to discover the intricate patterns of mosaic carpets, today completely unprotected from the elements, and could imagine the flow of life across their surfaces centuries before. The feet of family, friends and slaves traversed their surfaces, the remains of which, in solidarity, we crossed that day.

Paestum is famous for having the oldest, most complete Doric style temples in all of Italy, if not the world. The temples of Hera and Neptune (also known as Hera I and Hera II) are located next to each other toward the southern city gate, while the smaller Temple of Ceres is situated near Porta Aurea, the northern gate.

The Temple of Hera, the oldest of the three temples, was built about 550 BC in classic Doric style. Such a magnificent edifice today, if you can, try to comprehend that it has been there for 2,600 years. It has often been referred to in error as the *Basilica* because archaeologists mistakenly thought it was a Basilica, not in a religious connotation, but in contrast to today's use of the word, meaning a Roman public building in the language of archaeology. Today there is little doubt that it was dedicated to Hera thanks to inscriptions found on the temple. Hera (Roman name Juno), sister of Poseidon, was the goddess of marriage and an important deity. She was the wife of Zeus and Queen of the gods on Mount Olympus. Hera was revered as the sole Greek goddess who accompanied a woman through her life. In fact, her name translates to "Great Lady". This goddess blessed and protected a woman's marriage, brought fertility, protected her children, and helped her find financial security. Hera was, in short, the complete female, one-stop-shopping goddess. Ever wonder why the most popular month for weddings happens to be June? June, after her Roman name Juno, is the month named in honor of Hera.

Some distance away to the north lies the Temple of Athena (or Ceres), goddess of wisdom, known to the Romans as Minerva. It was the second temple built, circa 500 BC, and is the smallest of the three. It commands Paestum's highest ground, what there is of it, as temples dedicated to Athena did. Its followers continued worshipping there until the very end of ancient Paestum. As the decline became inevitable, and this being the high ground, the remaining population settled around this temple to avoid the encroaching marshlands. Later, when Christianity became dominant, the temple was converted into a Christian church as was the typical fate of pagan temples (like: the Pantheon in Rome, 125 AD) before it, too, was abandoned.

The last and largest of the great temples to be built, the Temple of Neptune (or Apollo or Hera II) dates from 470-460 BC and is the most complete of the three temples. Everything is intact except for the roof and some of its inner walls. Looking at it you would think you were on the Acropolis in Athens, gazing at the Parthenon.

At one point, I laid chest down on the pavement of the

Cardo Maximus, once the main north-south road through the city and served to connect the three great temples. Lying there I snapped a picture. Gone were the religious processions and wagon traffic that had been its past. What remained were flat, loosely-spaced, dark-colored stone slabs deeply grooved by centuries of passage and a lone wild dandelion asserting itself from between the stones. That day when the city awoke, it was shrouded in the mist of its ever present past, not the smoke from countless home-fires. And that day, evident from the presence of that lone, humble flower, it was clearly at peace— the gods had indeed been merciful.

March, 2008

**48. Dandelion on
Cardo Maximus, Paestum**

23

Fresca Air

Our knives glided through the heap of *ricotta fresca*, as light as a morning cobweb. We were like confectioners frosting little cakes as we spread the frothy, white as a lily, cheese across the pocked surface of crusty slabs of fresh newborn bread. I was primed to begin eating my adorned concoction right then but hesitated when Erminio, our lanky young waiter, encouraged us to top off each creation with the addition of one final ingredient, roasted hunks of tiny cherry peppers. It was the addition of the peppers which made this open faced *pièces de résistance* all the more sumptuous and exotic.

While wonderful is an understatement, heavenly is more in order. This delicacy alone was worth the trip to *Grillo D'Oro* (The Golden Cricket) since, all these months later, we still fondly recall our time there and the small adventures along the way.

It was a cool, grey October day. We were of a mind for soup. We had come to Bisaccia from our mountainside community of Calitri, not far to the south, with a quick exploratory segue through nearby Aquilonia. The countryside was dormant,

49. Grillo D'Oro Restaurant, Bisaccia

awaiting the coming winter rains. Already the farmlands that surrounded us had been prepared for the next season, evidenced by the furrows of harrowed soil, which joined the landscape to the horizon in every direction.

Rural Italians have always been nature conscious, always trustworthy stewards of the land from time immemorial. Equally, they have been very energy conscious. Today, nature and conservation combine in the average Italian to spawn a motive force to not only conserve to save his earthly planet, but also his Euros!

I was surprised for instance, when I noticed how long it took a clothes washer to do even the small load it held. It had something to do with a machine designed to substitute time for energy. By design, our machine doesn't even have a hot water connection. Actually, we should have done them by hand to really save, just as some of the locals still do. For drying, however, we rely on a handy wooden dowel rack out on the sun-porch, or as back-up, the little plasticized clothesline outside our bedroom window. Not wanting to waste either energy or money, Italian lifestyles have adapted to foster environmental sustainability, to control costs, and to seek renewable energy, while handicapping pollution. Need some practical evidence? Just go into a local store and notice that not until then will the proprietor turn on the lights.

At home, we talk a great story about renewable energy but in fact do little beyond resist its adaptation. This is especially so when it is on our doorstep, or as they say, "In my backyard". Take, for instance, the high profile wind farm proposed for Nantucket Sound off the coast of Massachusetts. Why would anyone object to harnessing the wind out there? But in these times, I've come to realize that the obvious is not always apparent, a slam-dunk, a sure thing. White can be black, and even an enormous benefit incapable of outweighing political power dominated by wealthy influence. Alliances in opposition have formed boasting slogans to fight to maintain the view and real estate values. Delaying tactics are concocted proclaiming the need to save wayward birds misfortunate enough to impinge on these *Cuisiniart* traps. To un-level the playing field further, legalistic snares are set to delay needed licensing in the monofilament of red tape. Like modern Don Quixote's, the opposition gird themselves for battle across a chess board spanning 25 square miles (6,500 hectares) of sound against the homely enemy, 130 turbines.

Wind, a source of energy that's inexhaustible, non-polluting, and secure, is found unacceptable, mainly due, when you get right down to it, to the fact that these windmills will be visible on the far horizon from the summer homes of the rich and powerful of Cape Cod's south shore. My guess is that when you are so rich that you can afford to live on the south shore, approaching $5 a gallon gasoline and ever-costly heating oil is irrelevant. So long as the turbines are out of sight, the well-to-do can put it out of their minds and continue their beautiful lives out of touch with the reality of today's energy costs and its consequences. No matter whence the wind blows, in my opinion, this stinks.

On the flip side of this too-true US reality, we found wind

50. Roadside wind turbines, Bisaccia

energy openly embraced by Italians. I wonder what, if anything, they objected to when the idea was first broached? Maybe they had a hereditary predisposition to them. For when they look off into the distance, as they do from their mountaintop perched towns, the turbines may have resembled some ancient Roman siege machine so germane to their landscape for so many centuries. In fact, the environs of Calitri sport these energy talismans as though they were wild mushrooms. Much, if not all, of our electricity comes from these twirligigs.

Indeed, up close, they are large metallic behemoths. On the road into Aquilonia, we had an opportunity to get near a few of these sentinels of the wind, as their machete blades were propelled by the wind. It was interesting to see how modern technology blended with tradition as forays of shotgun-toting hunters sauntered through the fields beneath them, their dogs out ahead scouring for birds, their noses close to the ground as if sensing for truffles. Above them, the silver skinned machines soared skyward sensing the winds.

Atop each slender stanchion, a streamlined cabin, concealing a generator and controls, swiveled to align its giant prop with the prevailing wind currents of the moment. From below, what appeared to be tiny antennae, undoubtedly approximating the length of a pole-vaulting shaft close-up, facilitated the receipt of distant commands to orient these monsters, even feather their blades when told to rest. While the wind blew sufficiently to satisfy their insatiable hunger, some were at rest when we approached. In what appeared to be phalanx regiments, pockets of these machines dappled the landscape as we moved on toward Bisaccia and the *Grillo D'Oro*, farther northward from Aquilonia across this high windswept plateau.

The family run *antica osteria, Grillo D'Oro,* served its first guests, no doubt coexisting even then with the *Luzzano* winds, way back in 1872 by offering them simple dishes of *la cucina contadina.* Loosely translated this means straightforward, unfussy peasant cooking. Inside, present became past for just a moment when, in the stone behind a modest bar, I spotted the date 1872 proudly showcased. The modern dining area was modestly sized. It arced around to the left from where we sat and

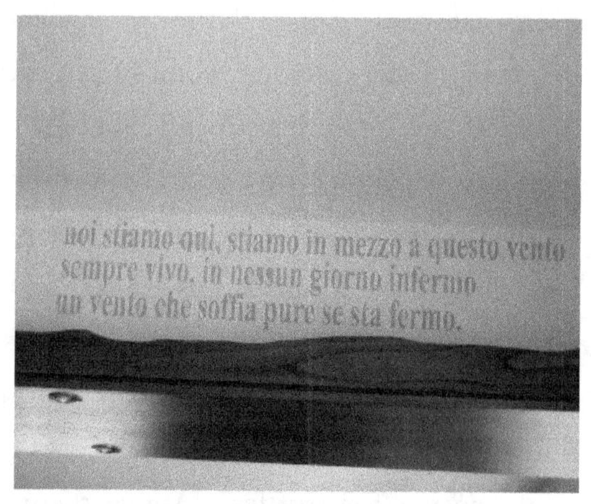

51. Grillo D'Oro ceiling poem to the winds, Bisaccia

was lit by repeating sets of windows. Tables of devout eaters filled its stone and tiled space. Attesting to their close kinship to the land, the clear air and wind, we found poetic script on the ceiling soffits, fittingly positioned directly above a long table of hunters, apparently just in from the hills. Roughly translated it read:

> *We are here, we are in the midst of this wind*
> *Always alive even on a still day*
> *A wind that blows even if we are still.*
> *In my town you see Puglia, the straw.*

While on a clear but windy day you might be able to spy distant Foggia in neighboring Puglia, our windblown souls were on the lookout for that comforting *cucina contadina*. The day we were fortunate enough to sample their lunchtime cuisine, it was the place to try steeping hot rustic soup made with sun-dried vegetables, in addition to a frittata and handmade pasta. Indeed, we tried our best to heartily accommodate the sumptuous offerings following the rarefied *ricotta fresca*, which served as our antipasto initiation to *Grillo D'Oro*. We followed our hearty soup with penne pasta, pointed like quill pens and tumbled in an authentic rabbit ragù judiciously coated with a snowstorm of *parmigiano reggiano*. A bottle of Campania Aglianico wine,

52. Maria Elena and Geraldina enjoying themselves

sporting its own Golden Cricket label, completed this midday repast. Instead of artful plate decoration, everything had been prepared in a way that highlighted the local ingredients. By the time we'd finished, our table had become a ransacked still-life portrait replete with empty bottles, cups, a few remaining peppers, a dollop of ricotta, spilled cheese and enough pane morsels to keep the scrape of a bread crumber well occupied. Complimentary glasses of *limoncello* finally quenched our appetites. *Finito!* We were sated, close to spill-over-full, when we made our goodbyes.

We emerged from *Grillo D'Oro* to be greeted once again by the now familiar stands of wind turbines, this particular batch on a neighboring ridge beyond the parking lot. Driving away, I couldn't resist stopping to take one last picture, this time of a middle-aged man standing on a nearby street corner. I'd been attracted by his attire. His smile also beckoned my approach.

He wore a cap, to me reminiscent of something worn by an American civil war soldier. His jacket was of muted greens with tan and black blotches in a camouflage style similar to a military fatigue jacket. Beneath blue-jean trousers, his boots, lugging what I suspected was mud from his last foray, finished him off. Beside him, leaning against the wall and protecting its contents from damage, was a worn rifle case. With a nod first to my camera and then toward him, he smiled in agreement to my primal communication. I took the shot and inquired where he was headed (*Dove stai andando?*). No birds for this intrepid fellow, he'd leave them to the windmills! He was going wild boar (*cinghiale*) hunting in the neighboring chestnut forests. A hunter in the truest sense, one man attempting to defeat wild nature juxtaposed against the creations of other men attempting to tame the very breath of nature.

We continued on to Calitri among the mechanical sentinels, saying our goodbyes to each through our rear view mirror and to yet another brief

53. The wild boar hunter, Bisaccia

interlude with intimate Italian culture and its shiny, bristling technology.

When someday I finally relax, settle back and reminisce over a lifetime of things done and others unfinished, maybe even take time to wonder what jobs I'd missed out on (like 'second grip' or 'gaffer' I see scroll by in movie credits), I will make room to remember moments like these, tucked away almost as a bride with her hope-chest does—a memory to be re-awakened on another day, at another time, in another place.

For in Italy, which I do not yet truly know but which still has a pull on me, where time is a continuum and where life doesn't move with breakneck speed, you can make memories as in no other place in the universe. Verde may have said it best when he penned . . . "You may have the universe if I may have Italy!" We'd made an afternoon of it, let it play out, blowing in the wind to the rhythm of the land in search of soup, and in the process formed airy memories of food, hunters, and enough windmills to last our lifetimes.

June, 2008

24

Angela and the Mayor

Recently, Maria Elena and I had the pleasure of attending a family wedding in Tiverton, Rhode Island. Shortly afterward, at the reception, we experienced another surprising pleasure when we meet another couple who shared with us a true family story in courage. This is when we were introduced to Angela Rainone, who, though absent that day is even now the courageous heroine of this tale. While the basic storyline is correct, I have taken liberty to embellish it somewhat to flesh-out the characters and events, and for this, I too ask forgiveness.

He knew the law, the situation, and that he somehow had to protect his son. Fortunately, as the mayor, he was the law in Panni, but beyond its tiny jurisdiction in this corner of Basilicata, not far distant from Calitri, was a much greater world with regulations and reach far beyond his power to control – in this case, the power and rule of the central government in *Roma*.

How could he circumvent the official dictates of the Italian government, which now directed that his son, Michele Rainone, immediately report for military duty in this, a time of war? He had pondered the issue for weeks since the official directive had arrived. A furtive scheme, born from necessity, began to emerge. He had reached a decision.

While the July 1916 letter from the capital said that one, Michele Rainone, must report for induction by mid-September, his response would be to substitute another man, one with the same name, though not his relation. Who would be the wiser? No one would know of his subterfuge. His son would remain in Panni, safe from the world and the war outside.

A letter had been sent to the surrogate Michele and the business, he thought, concluded. But in only three days a crisis had ensued. He had underestimated the determination and raw persistence of Michele's mother, Angela Rainone. Herself but a widow, she had literally positioned herself between her son and the mayor's plan.

Saturday

Angela arrived at his *comune* office early and had asked his secretary to speak with the mayor. He had put her off, suspecting her motives and thinking she would soon tire and go away. He was wrong, for she stayed around all that day, sitting quietly in the hallway, her back to the window, outside his office in silent protest. An icon of motherly resolve with a maternal instinct for her child, she had deflected each announcement that the mayor was unavailable only to counter that she would remain there until he could see her.

When he left for the *reposo* that day, she was still there. A standoff was clearly underway. Passers-by in the town hall were beginning to notice. Gradually, people began to talk. When he returned later that same day, she approached him. With stiletto precision she simply said, "*So che la legge. So quello che state facendo a mio figlio.*" (I know the law. I know what you are doing to my son.) Aloof, and with an air that he didn't grasp her meaning, he made a feeble retreat into his sanctuary of his office.

Sunday

He thought about it all night, turning events over and over in his mind as often as he sleeplessly tossed in his bed. How could this simple woman have known of the law, which said that the only son of a widow could not be drafted? She therefore knew that the letter was intended for another—no doubt his son of the same name.

Word of Angela's sit-in and variations on the reason for it had spread rapidly through the town. He thought that even the parish priest during Mass that day looked at him accusingly as he sat with other town elders in their special box by the altar. His sermon about the example of Abraham and Isaac was like sand in his growing wound. He, not God, had found the substitute lamb to sacrifice. Looking about now and then with brief stolen glances, he hadn't found Angela in church; he knew where she must be. Even the *buòngiornos* he received were few, hollow, and somehow spoken with something less than courtesy. He feared she had become a poster child to his chicanery. In this instance, he was correct.

Monday

When Mayor Rainone entered the local cafe that morning, as he did every morning for his *caffè*, there were whispers in the eyes of the townspeople. He knew, Angela knew, and now it was clear, they knew. Even his son had come to him the evening before. "I know you are doing this to protect me, father. You have always taught me to do right, and now father, you must do what is right, no matter how hard it is for you."

His son's words weighed on him throughout another long night. Indeed he had done this out of paternal instinct, all for his son, just as Angela was acting on her own son's behalf. The difference was that righteousness was on her side. He'd known this for weeks, and had managed to suppress it. Now he realized he had to set things right again, for his son, himself, the surrogate soldier, Angela, and the people of Panni. He knew then what he had to do.

Her shadow on the floor announced that she was still there even before he rounded the corner outside his office that morning. He could tell from the personal belongings, which now surrounded her, that she had again been encamped there through the night in vigil to her cause. He approached her as she sat there quietly on the bench outside his office absorbed in her thoughts, which rejected any sense of the futility of her actions and sustained her in humble revolt. She rose at his approach. Her eyes and his connected as he solemnly said, "You can have your son back and hopefully I, someday, will have your forgiveness."

It was done. A lone but courageous woman armed only with

the truth and a mother's resolve had dared to openly challenge authority and had won. Some in Panni would sleep well that night, long, long ago.

Postscript

Michele Rainone, who knew right from wrong, died in the Battle of Caporetto in 1917 for his country, his village, and his father.

Angela Rainone, revered by her neighbors the rest of her life, lived to the age of 95.

Mayor Guiliano Rainone was never re-elected. Angela attended his funeral.

Michele Rainone, Angela's son, immigrated to America and was killed in a hit and run accident in Rhode Island. Angela never attended his funeral. This fact is true.

We live, we work, we love and hopefully in the days we have, do great and honorable things.

July, 2008

25

Castagne Everywhere and a Few Americans for Good Measure

I was in Calitri, in Mario's Cafe in fact, when I first noticed the flyers on the countertop advertising an upcoming *sagra* (festival) in Montella. When I checked, I found that Montella sits on the side of the mountains overlooking the Calore River quite a few hills and river valleys from Calitri. Situated to the west of Calitri, it is one of several towns clustered in that area along with Nusco, Bagnoli and tiny Cassano. All are not too far from of the main road between Lioni and

54. Author, Antonio, Maria Elena, and Carl, Montella

Avellino. Surprisingly, Montella is one of the largest towns of Irpinia, with approximately 9,000 inhabitants.

I also came across the fact that Montella was founded around the 4th century BC. Because of its defensive qualities, the Romans made it a *municipium*, a distinct, self-governing, city-state in the region. Today, a town's defensive nature wouldn't even be a consideration, but then, nothing much mattered without security then. In 571 AD, as part of the Lombard Kingdom, it became a Longobard fortress, after which its ownership changed hands among powerful and wealthy families for the next 1,000 years until the downfall of feudalism in the 18th century.

Inspired by the French Revolution, the movement for Italian unification, and Giuseppe Garibaldi and his 1000 red shirt volunteer army, that eventually liberated southern Italy, Montella threw-in its support for the *Risorgimento* (Rising Again), the movement to unify Italy, culminated in the establishment of the Kingdom of Italy in 1861. Success had its drawbacks however. The newly-formed, yet weak central government could not quickly supplant the control of former Austrian and French rule. In the resulting vacuum, Montella suffered from bandits who operated in mountain areas throughout the area. I guess they had finally experienced their own security concerns.

What makes Montella so special and therefore a magnet for visitors, at least in October of each year, isn't a history based on some miraculous apparition or some celebrated ruin. No, its notoriety rests in the fact that Montella chestnuts (*castagne*) are among the most renowned in Italy. In fact, the old Latin name for this sweet nut, *castanea*, is the source of the fruit's name. But be forewarned, don't go there and say that this fruit is anything less than the absolute best in the entire world.

What more reason do you need for a fall *Sagra della Castagna di Montella?* Reason enough for us to want to visit during the *sagra.* Along with the festival that year would also be the 11th market exhibition of traditional products. In addition to chestnuts, the hills of the *Alta Valle del Calore*, surrounding the town, are also famous for their black truffles and mushrooms, which can be found year round. Ah, chestnuts and more!

Now, the Montella variety of chestnut should not be confused with horse-chestnuts (also called buckeyes), that are superficially similar to the Montella variety. Gosh, I remember chestnuts as a kid. I was always able to find the small, un-hulled, prickly capsules, sometimes with three nuts inside, strewn across the ground under a West Street tree on my way to grammar school. These buckeyes were easy pickings for anyone looking for a supply, not to roast, but to toss at various targets of opportunity along the way. Undoubtedly, mine were of the lesser buckeye variety.

Shenanigans aside, chestnuts in Montella are serious business. Today, over 100 area companies are licensed to work with chestnuts, they being the main source of income for Montella and the surrounding area, and accounting for 60% of Avellino province's production.

Chestnuts abound in the forests that surround the town. It's interesting to note that chestnuts, originally from Asia Minor, have been known to this region since the 4th century BC. In fact, in southern Europe during the Middle Ages (approx 400–1,500 AD), entire forest-dwelling communities, having limited access to wheat flour, relied on chestnuts as their main source of carbohydrates.

Chestnuts have enjoyed legal protection in Italy beginning way back with the Longobards in the 6th century. Today there is a legal framework of protected designation, with the aim of enhancing and promoting products of a specific character. It is known as a Protected Geographical Indication (IGP). Today, the Montella chestnut is certified IGP due to the recognition of its unique characteristics, which distinguish it from similar products in the same category. Their taste vary slightly from one to the next but in general is somewhat sweet and certainly unique.

Chestnut-based recipes are making a comeback in Italian cuisine as part of the trend toward the rediscovery of

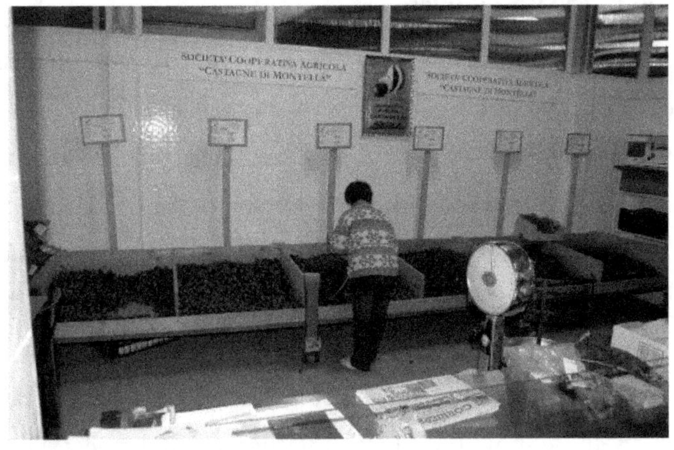

55. Chestnut warehouse, Montella

traditional dishes. One important use of chestnuts is to grind them into flour, which is then used to make bread, cakes, even pasta. You can't imagine to what uses they put these odd fruits. They can be eaten boiled or roasted, even candied. Try *castagne fresche* (fresh), *castagne essiccate in guscio* (dried), *castagne essiccate sgusciate* (shelled), *castagne del Prete* (chestnut of the priest), *farina di Castagne* (flour) and *confettura di castagne* (jam). Chestnut gelato? I'm not sure, but I wouldn't put it past them.

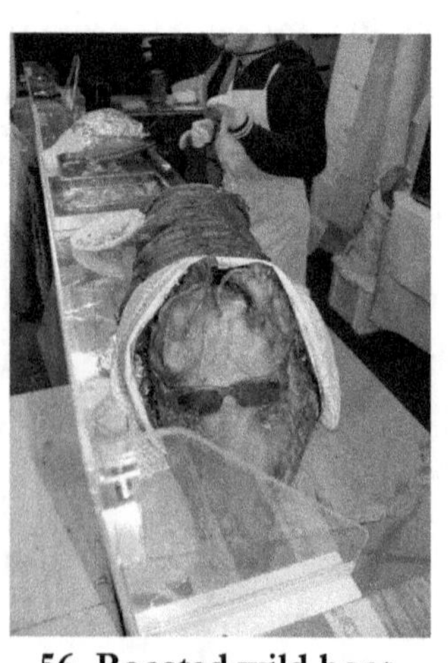

56. Roasted wild boar with sunglasses

Before we arrived at the festival, we first stopped at the Chestnut Cooperative housed in a big warehouse just outside of town. It was evident that this was indeed big business. You could buy various grades of chestnuts there by the bushel, or should I say, kilogram. They even shipped worldwide.

Once in town, we found too small a space to shoehorn our car into and walked the few streets to the center of town. Almost immediately we took the opportunity to sample one of the sumptuous traditional products offered, this being a pork *panini* sandwich made from a whole roasted pig on display (one wore sunglasses, another was festooned in classic caricature with an apple in its mouth) and if that was not sweet enough, we also sampled the local nougat *torroni* sweets. There was also the famous *ricotta mantecata* cheese (ricotta cream cheese) to

57. Scraping melted caciocavallo cheese, Montella

sample, which Montella is also known for. One booth that evening was particularly interesting. It featured something I'd never seen before. Using what looked like *caciocavallo* cheese dangling from cords over white hot embers, I watched as the now satiny soft cheese was first scraped from its host and then smeared across the pocked surface of crusty bread, oozing into every pore. *Delizioso*!

I had just returned from investigating the insides of a local butcher shop and remarked to Maria Elena that I'd bet we were the only Americans in town when someone nearby overheard me and quickly introduced himself. He was Carl from Venice, Florida. He sported a leather bomber jacket with fur collar and the international ID of all tourists, a camera, dangling from his neck (who am I to talk). Following a few *Mi piacere's* of introduction to his cousin of local stock, Carl began to extol the virtues of, of all places, Costa Rico. It seems he had just returned and was definitely high on its praises. He'd gone there for dental surgery and as he explained, with its modern facilities, excellent service and low costs, it was 'the' place to go when you were in that market. He'd become their overly exuberant, walking, talking, shiny teeth flashing, one man advertisement for the place, at least there in Montella.

It was only moments after saying goodbye to Carl that we met a large group of Americans from Virginia. Was everyone American in some sort of Disney Epcot Center, Italian setting switcheroo? We chatted about the whats, whys, and where you've beens for a few minutes and learned that this cheery group, as in past years, had come specifically for the festival, just as Carl had. The troop of Virginians was soon overshadowed by the sounds of a local band just starting to perform nearby. Soon, people all around us swayed in primal thrall to their rhythmic beat and melancholy voices. Given the fires, the night, the throaty voices and earthy cadence, it was easy to imagine being transported thousands of years into the past, no doubt akin to similar firesides, whether Longobard or brigand.

Leaving Montella behind, we stopped off for dinner at the *Conte Restaurante and Pizzeria*, a mountainside restaurant not far from Nusco. I doubt I could ever recount how we got there exactly, or even someday retrace the route even in broad daylight. For a while, in fact, I had a hard time believing there could be anything anywhere along that out in the boonies dirt road. As we continued to turn and climb, what eventually emerged was a parking area, quite full in fact, and a one-story building opposite with a series of sprawling wings, no doubt a response over time to its growing popularity. Once we were served, it became clear that the next time we visited, we'd surely find the road paved in response to its continued success. What was important was not the building, its decor, the music or who was in the chairs but what was on the table. Divine pizza! You know the kind—thin, fire-baked crust, mozzarella slices, pesto, a little garlic, pignoli nuts, drizzled olive oil, and a few scattered basil leaves for good measure.

Again, this was the last place I expected to find a group of Americans but there they where, a whole, noisy table full. This was a single family from Philadelphia. To be precise, it was restaurateur, John Varallo, from *Restaurante Pesto* in what remains of the 'little Italy' section of Philadelphia. Like the others, he too had returned for the festival, as he had many times in past years, this time with some of his sons.

Our idyllic sojourn over, we returned to Calitri. No dress rehearsal, this had been our first, real, Italian *sagra*. Some rarefied world of the true aficionado? Not really. It was just a down to earth, local, good time with a timeless quality, centuries old, and telling from the number of Americans, no well kept secret.

August, 2008

**58. The Lancelot Hotel's
common patio area, Rome**

26

A Roman Holiday

It was all a ruse! Instead of just proposing, straight out, that we stay in Rome a few days, Maria Elena finessed the idea by reasoning with me about our luggage. We only had one hour to make our Paris to Rome connection. On that basis, she schemed that, if our suitcases didn't make it following our arrival in Rome, due to the tight schedule or any unforeseen delays, maybe it would be better to plan an overnight or two in Rome just to be on the safe side. After all, wouldn't it be easier for the airlines to find us and deliver our luggage to us while in Rome verses trying to track us down in Calitri? How many days would that take . . . days without luggage? She definitely has the gift.

I could have countered that we should think more positively, especially since Air France does this every day, but in the back of my mind I liked the idea of a few days of leisure in Rome before moving on to Calitri. We had been to Rome a few times before and there were always new places to visit, as well as a city full of fabulous restaurants. Thinking back on it now, it kind of reminds me of a scene from the movie, *My Big Fat Greek Wedding* when another Maria says to her daughter, Toula,

"Let me tell you something, Toula. The man is the head, but the woman is the neck. And she can turn the head any way she wants."[1] Needless to say, there was no problem with our luggage and we stayed on, two days in Rome!

We had reservations at the *Lancelot Hotel* located on *Via Capo D'Africa*, just a few blocks from the Coliseum. I'd describe it as a boutique hotel and reasonably priced, especially when you consider you are situated practically in downtown Rome. Following our pleasant stay there, we can now highly recommend it.

It has a few especially nice features. One was our exclusive use, both nights, of a common patio area on the sixth floor, close to our room. Apparently, no other guests were interested or aware of its availability. From this vantage point, we could easily see the venerable Coliseum off to our left through the assortment of plants, which defined the patio's perimeter. This was even more spectacular by night, when the Coliseum's pocked, naked surface, rising above intervening rooftops, was ghostly illuminated.

One late afternoon, following a busy day about the city, we decided to eat in. A nearby market afforded the opportunity to pick up some staples like wine, cheese, a few finger-length *sopressata* salamis, *pane*, even some olives and marinated artichokes, all of which we enjoyed outside in the refreshing evening air of the patio. Down the way, on another hotel rooftop, an Irish wedding was underway. Don't ask how I knew.

---

1 *My Big Fat Greek Wedding.* HBO Home Video, 2003.

With the Coliseum, sounds of a Dionne Warwick recording wafting in from the wedding, and a Vespa engine in the street below as company, we completed our dinner table with wine glasses, a corkscrew, and a candlestick willingly provided by our hosts.

The next night, we had opportunity to sample our first ever zucchini blossoms. We had read some very favorable comments about a place named *Restaurante Le Naumachie di Micheli Alfredo*, just blocks away on *Via Celimontana*. I'd confirmed these glowing reports independently with Mrs Kahn, the *Lancelot's* amicable owner. Her response, when I asked her for a restaurant recommendation, was to vector us to the *Naumachie*, even though her own establishment served dinner nightly. Following her directions, we found this gem on a nearby street corner located between our hotel and the Coliseum, only a short walk and a few turns away. What a simple, unpretentious find it was.

The meaning of its name is particularly fitting. *Le Naumachie* was an imitation sea battle staged in a Roman amphitheatre, like the nearby Coliseum, which was flooded for the occasion. The combatants were usually prisoners of war or convicts who fought from trireme ships until one side was defeated. The first *naumachia* re-enactment on record was hosted by Julius Caesar in 46 BC, on a lake which he constructed in Rome's Campus Martius, to depict a battle between the Tyrian and Egyptian fleets. Later, Augustus staged a *naumachia* between Athenians and Persians in a basin newly constructed on a bank of the Tiber. The symbol for the restaurant, embossed on the tablecloths and the T-shirt sported by our waiter, Daniel, was in fact a colorful trireme under full sail. Unfortunately, neither was available for sale (no pun intended!).

We shared our long table with an antique dealer whose shop was near the Spanish Steps and his friend, a TV sales and repairman. Our conversation began with menu questions following the arrival of their interesting meals and a comment about the ruby ring I was wearing. They had dissected a softball sized serving of buffalo mozzarella, and on seeing this, we also had to try one. One was plenty for the two of us. That incomparable buffalo mozzarella flavor, oozing with its milky whey fluid, is like none other.

Unaware of the availability of the ever-elusive zucchini blossom until our table-mates were served a platter, we again followed suit. We knew what they were but had until that moment never had an opportunity to sample them. I enjoyed them immensely, but Mare could detect a slightly fishy aftertaste. Come to find out, she was absolutely correct. I theorized that they had somehow used oil tainted from frying fish, but Daniel set me straight when he informed us that the traditional Roman style for the deep fried blossoms included anchovy in the batter. What taste buds Maria Elena has (she can also out-smell me).

For a later course, I selected a comforting bowl of *bucatini* pasta and I was glad I did. This style of pasta was new to me and I don't think it would be easily find in Calitri. Thankful, we later found that both *Joséphine's Centro Market* and the CONAD Supermarket in Calitri carried it. These hollow, cord-like strands of pasta were sturdy yet tender in the accompanying cheese and pancetta red sauce, which clung to its enhanced surface area. While I savored each mouthful, Maria Elena enjoyed a white pizza with garlic, cheese and pignoli nuts. Our meals lustily consumed, Daniel presented us complementary *limoncello* aperitifs. Unless *Le Naumachie* franchises itself and establishes itself in Calitri, we will dearly miss this unassuming neighborhood eatery.

Le Naumachie was definitely a respite from the numerous tourist traps that abound in Rome. It offers simple dishes from a limited menu but more than compensates with personal attention to every guest. For our part, all we needed to do was engage . . . with the waiter, or as in our case, with fellow patrons. The presence of typical Romans, like our table-mates, reinforced the notion that true Roman fare could be found only a few streets away from the tumult of busy tourist thoroughfares and their high prices. Clearly, these locals were out, not for a sea battle, but for a wonderful traditional meal, right down to the detail of including pungent anchovy in the recipe. Enough about food though. We now needed to burn off some of those calories, especially pasta boy. We didn't realize it then, but a major calorie buster was definitely in store for us.

The next morning, we made leisurely rounds of *Piazza Navona* and *Campo de Fiori*, but our real objective was the dome of Saint Peter's Basilica. We had been to the Vatican on two previous occasions, but this time we wanted to enjoy the spectacular view of the Vatican grounds and downtown Rome only available from this unique vantage point. The domed top of the basilica, designed and started by Michelangelo to soar 448 feet above the floor of the basilica to the tip of its external cross, is officially the highest point in Rome. We wanted to stand beneath that cross and experience a sight that had been denied even the likes of Michelangelo himself.

Once we passed through what I refer to as the modesty police tent, where vigilant church staff members scan for over exposed legs, bare shoulders, risqué halter tops and who knows what else (and they call that work!), we headed for the access to the dome. You had a choice—for 5 Euros you could take the stairs, while for 7 Euros, an elevator. We opted for the elevator, naively thinking (more like not thinking it through at all) that we would emerge on the circular overlook at the base of the Lantern, which is what that crowning piece on the very top of the dome is called. Unfortunately, the elevator deposits you on the roof at the base of the dome. Little did we realize that this is the tallest dome in the world. We were going to find

59. Lantern atop St. Peter's, Rome

this out the hard way, on foot.

I should have realized that no elevator could navigate the narrow, arched confines inside the brick, double-shell construction of this unique dome. Michelangelo hadn't the technical help of someone like Galileo (who, by the way, was but three days old when Maestro Buonarotti died) to invent an escalator, which would have been a wonderful addition to his design. Instead, it would have to be 'a stairway to heaven'.

60. Maria Elena ascending the Vatican dome staircase, Rome

We began our assent, or should I say assault, single file. 327 steps lay before us. It was nice enough at first, but soon, because the dome is really ovoid in shape, rising steeply at first before arching over toward the top, we began to feel squeezed between the inner and outer arching surfaces at just about the time our legs were giving out. I must add this was not a jaunt for the claustrophobic. The ever narrowing, curved space was also hot by this time. You breathed the heat. There were small, barred window openings where you could hesitate every so often before moving on, but that was about it in way of a reprieve. The relentless stream of fellow view seekers, behind us, made it impossible to change your mind, reverse course and ask for a refund. Believe me, the idea did occur to both of us. There was no way out but up, toward the heavens.

Wall mounted cameras monitored progress. We wondered aloud what they would do if someone actually collapsed. Would religious indulgences be granted if you survived this pilgrimage? By this time, the outer surface was touching my shoulder. I recall having to lean right to keep clear. We didn't know it, but about then we were approaching the top. At this point, we changed our pedestrian mode of transportation. Now began a sprint to the top via a circular staircase. It featured the tightest spiral I'd ever seen with a rope toward the center supposedly for a stable grip. Did I say stable? *Santa Maria!*

Eventually, we breached the sunlight onto the circular gallery surrounding the base of the Lantern to join a host of fellow, recovering, vertical trekkers. Above us were an intensely blue sky and the basilica's crowning crucifix, purported to contain a fragment of the True Cross and a relic of St. Andrew. It was one of those places that pulls the awe from inside you. The word spectacular is quite inadequate to describe the 360° panorama. It was as if we were flying 500 feet above the Eternal City, with the granite expanse of Bernini's Saint Peter's Square as our departure runway. Where else might you go to glimpse an entire country? Around us stretched Rome, a study in beauty and abundance, cradled within the palm of the distant Sabine Mountains and Alban Hills. It was easy to identify the saucer-shaped Pantheon, Hadrian's Mausoleum on the Tiber (today known as *Castle Sant'Angelo* of *Angels and Demons* fame), and the monument to Victor Emmanuel II by

61. View from the lantern, Rome

the Forum. Surrounding us on the sides and to our rear were the Vatican Museum, the roof of the Sistine Chapel and the manicured Vatican gardens, including the Fountain of the Eagles. We'd become soaring eagles ourselves!

Now recovered from our cardiovascular workout, we easily descended from our perch by an alternate route, this time with gravity on our side. Once again, we emerged onto the flat expanse of the roof, dotted with its many small cupolas and guard houses. We were beckoned by a very welcoming refreshment stand adjacent to a gift shop. Someone had thought through this trek. Two refreshing drinks, a postcard, and an elevator ride later, we were once again on terra firma, inside the Vatican, mission accomplished and all without receiving "The Last Rites". It had been an experience of biblical purport; Jacob's Ladder combined with Dante's Devine Comedy and a dash of the Inferno.

We made our way across the sprawling colonnaded piazza in front of Saint Peter's, pausing every so often to look back up at the Lantern, that lofty height where we had just been. After a cross-town bus ride, we were back at the *Lancelot Hotel.* Now very tired and hot, we sought the comfort of Havana Club rum with cokes in the coolness of their cozy bar. Again, as in our patio experience, it was just the two of us as sole occupants of a tiny, shabby-chic bar in far off Rome, that Eternal City.

It was good to have stayed the extra days, for time enjoyed is never really time wasted. In our brief stay, we had seen Rome in a different way, from different vantage points. We really hadn't needed to stay. Later that night, as we packed our suitcases, I smiled inwardly. It had been a ruse, but by whom? Without voicing it, we both silently knew Rome would be a delicious distraction and a chance to make new holiday memories . . . nothing whatsoever to do with luggage gone astray. In reality, it turned out to be all about a small, private, radiant with green patio, a jewel of a local restaurant, and that eternal staircase to heaven.

Again, without really thinking about it, as we busied ourselves, arranging the items in our suitcases, something had been forever rearranged in us. A Roman holiday will do that.

November, 2008

**62. View from St. Peter's square
toward where we'd been**

27

Surprises Along the Road Home

Our brief stay in Rome was over. We were off again, next destination Calitri. All told, we had been away from our adopted mountaintop community going on ten months. Arriving at this idyllic respite in the Campania hills would be like coming home, like gorging on a feast . . . hour to hour of welcome, contentment, rest, profound quietness and a general sense of satisfaction. It would not be like previous visits, for this time we knew what to expect, where things were, the ancient rhythm of the place and our place in it. We were eager to get there and begin an adventure of existence.

But first we had to get ourselves out of Rome. This is no small feat considering the maze of congested traffic, *senso unico* (one way) signs and scooter assaults on both flanks that we had to navigate, but not to worry, for we had Margaret along.

Who might Margaret be? Well, she is relatively new to travel with us, although now a steady companion. Unfortunately, at times, she can be most talkative, like one of those notorious back-seat drivers we've all experienced at one time or another, purveyor of road savvy seemingly effortlessly forthcoming,

especially when uninvited. To avoid any hard feelings, we let—
no, it is more like insist—that Margaret sit right up front with
us. She is a petite missy too, much less than a size 0 so there is
no problem with room in the front seat. Truth of the matter
is, Margaret's full name is Margaret N. Garmin, where the 'N'
stands for Nuvi. Let me fess-up. Margaret is really a Garmin,
Nuvi model 270 GPS receiver, fully preloaded with maps
of Italy. She comes by her royal sounding moniker because
she speaks with a British accent and thus we christened her
Margaret.

Margaret came into her own beginning at the downtown
Rome train station where we picked up our rental. Without a
hiccup, she expertly guided us back to the *Lancelot Hotel* where
we'd stayed, to retrieve our luggage. A few button pushes
later, we were on our way to Calitri with a planned detour to
the town of Taurasi to sample some of its celebrated *vino* of
the same name. We weren't even out of Rome when Maria
Elena declared Margaret her new best friend! She loved this
new contraption, however it worked. Mare was now free from
her seemingly lifetime, passenger seat job of reading maps
and taking the heat for missed turns and otherwise assorted
navigational missteps and mayhem. Gone were the hours
of wrong turns. She was now totally into management of
Margaret. We soon learned to listen to Margaret's directions for
it was unwise to disregard her guidance. Mare would council,
"Listen to Margaret", frequently. There were some initial
misunderstandings though. Because we sometimes travel on
unpaved Italian roads, I'd granted permission, in one of the

menus, for her to use un-surfaced roads. I soon realized this was a mistake. I thought the use of an unpaved road would be offset by my additional selection of 'fastest route', but once we departed the *Autostrada* and approached Taurasi, Margaret exercised her off-road prerogative and also our suspension. I'd chosen unpaved roads, not roads in complete disrepair! How could she have even known of these cattle trails through the paddocks? We saw yet another side of Italy that afternoon. We still managed to emerge in Taurasi, though not before a brief, first-gear tour through a vineyard along a white, sun-cracked dirt road with the added intrigue of washed-out gullies every now and then. Definitely not the fastest route nor the only route, I'm sure. British royalty aside, I had a serious talk with Margaret afterwards.

I'd wanted to visit Taurasi ever since first learning of its precious purple nectar from our sommelier friend, Rufus. Taurasi is in the heart of Campania, which I've learned is an amalgam of the Italian words *compagno* (companion) and *pane* (bread). Campania's underlying meaning then is "a companion with whom we break bread". We were this day, however, in search of a companion to share wine, since Margaret doesn't drink. Had I stumbled on something new here, *Campavino?*

The little town of Taurasi, headquarters for this DOCG designated wine, was mentioned by the historian Livy, but the Aglianico (pronounced ahi-YAH-nee koo) grape from which it is made has been cultivated since before Rome even existed. This was long before the Celts, living way to the north in the Piedmont home of today's Barolo wine, even knew what wine was. Though things get hazy at this point, historians think the grape may have been introduced by the Greeks as *Hellenica*. Long story even shorter, this name gradually mutated from *Hellanica* to, sometime in the 15th century, become *Aglianico*.

Taurasi wine is sometimes referred to as the *Barolo of the*

63. Waiting for a wine delivery, Taurasi

South. It is built for the long haul and I'm told ages well for up to 15-20 years, though I could never contain myself, let alone the wine, that long. The bouquet of this spell-casting wine is crammed full of all those aromas I read about but lack the distinctive mature nose, large as it is, to personally differentiate. I just know from drinking it that I enjoy it. After all, isn't that what wine is for? Taste this ruby fluid and you are immediately enveloped in an elegant, full-bodied yet 'smoooooth' wash of tannins.

We found our way to *Via Municipio*, which from its location looked to be the main street of Taurasi. It extended from

Piazza Padre Pio to the steps of the local medieval hamlet. We had arrived during the rest period, so there were few souls about. We parked by a local bar, which thankfully appeared open from the presence of a group of men seated around a white, plastic patio table playing cards. The sound of their knuckles slapping the table as they played out their hands and their equally expressive comments testified to their seriousness and sense of one-upsmanship. This seemed as good a place and time as any to inquire about Taurasi wine.

Things were improving immensely, for it just so happened that one of the bystanders was a nephew of Antonio Caggiano, the patriarch of Taurasi wine development in the area and whose wines are today the prestigious symbol of Irpinian viticulture. Following my inquiry, he produced a cell phone, and in a matter of minutes another relative arrived on a scooter and asked how many bottles we'd like! A couple *Moretti* beers later, he was back with a carton of label-less bottles from his personal stock bungeed to the back fender. We had struck pay-dirt and all for only a few Euros. Only a few weeks ago, in Chicago, I noted it selling for $86 a bottle!

Because of the time of day, *Cantine Antonio Caggiano* was closed, but on a chance, our new friend called anyway. Our luck continued. Antonio would meet us at his home, open his cantina and take us on a private tour—Saints be praised! We left Margaret in the car as timeout for her recent behavior, which we hadn't fully recovered from yet, and walked the few streets to Antonio's home. We found it easily, just as described.

It lay within an ornately accented iron and stone-walled

compound dominated by a tall shading pine. It was a hot day, approaching if not already in the 90's, yet the wealth of plants, the shade and red flowering vases throughout the garden evoked the sense of a refreshing oasis. The gate lay open, expecting us. To the side of the house at table with friends, sharing wine, was Antonio who rose to greet us. He was a balding, elderly gentleman, short in stature though wiry and vigorous in appearance. His face was heavily tanned, undoubtedly from years of work in the fields. His complexion served to accent his closely kept white beard. He sported the stub of a cigar more inside his mouth than was ever visible. We were soon

64. Cantine Antonio Caggiano, Taurasi

off to his cantina. Surprisingly, it was only a street away. We didn't realize it then but we were in store for many surprises. We should have been forewarned by the structure we passed next to his home. While from a distance it would appear to many to be a one-car garage, this garage had been converted into a chapel complete with brightly colored ceiling and wall frescos.

The stone and brick building he led us to was multistoried and from all evidence, new, yet it emoted a look and feel hundreds of years old. Its stone and bricked exterior was beautiful just to look at, reminiscent of something you might commonly see in Tuscany. A large boulder engraved *Cantine Antonio Caggiano* left little doubt that we had arrived. Our next surprise was that it proved to be much more than a typical wine tasting cantina since much was invisible, below ground. It revealed itself to be a combination photo gallery, museum, wine cellar and, can you believe, even a church.

One of Antonio's many talents includes photography, evident in the hallway leading to a subterranean labyrinth. This hallway was lined with his photos, one of which was of his mother. From here our descent into an underworld of amazement began. Through some inexplicable means, he had created an amazingly beautiful stone world of cavernous grand halls, arches, barrel-vaulted ceilings and grottos connected by dimly lit corridors, which seemed to stretch on and on in maze-like fashion. Antonio walked ahead of us to turn on lights and dissolve the darkness as we commenced to explore the unique world he'd created.

Here was the home of 'the' benchmark of Irpinia's finest wine, ruby red *Taurasi Macchia Dei Goti*. It is the only red wine from the Campania region awarded the DOCG distinction of quality. Room after room was filled with French oak barriques, artwork in themselves. Beginning at the cork on the top side of each barrel, a stain, like a purple painted rivulet, ran down the side from dribble after dribble of wine extracted for periodic testing. There were hallways of gated locked grottos containing a treasure trove of wines. In addition to *Macchia Dei Goti* there were piles of reclining, modern-styled

**65. Cantine Antonio Caggiano wine
storage grotto, Taurasi**

Salae Domini and younger *Taurasi* bottled reds, all made from 100% Aglianico grapes. Each stash had a small sign atop the heap stating its name and vintage —it amounted to an amazing wealth of bottled sunshine.

A charming panoply of artwork, call them 'little people', lay just ahead, for in an adjacent room we found ourselves in a Lilliputian world of significant miniaturization. All around us there unfolded a landscape of diminutive woodsmen, farmers, shepherds and maidens drawn from the unlimited world of Antonio's imagination. They were all carved of wood and were, at most, about 15 inches in height. Among them, one figure surprisingly stood out. There in the midst of this cavalcade was a caricature with the face of our host, Antonio, pulling a cart of wine bottles and waving! This pastoral procession

66. Cantine Antonio Caggiano little people figurines, Taurasi

spread across the floor. Their passage interrupted with tools, bottles, and various antique farm implements. They were all apparently headed to the far end of the cavern where a nativity scene replete with animals, a Madonna and a baby Jesus waited atop a slope composed of dusty wine bottles, knurly ancient vines and overturned demijohns. Again, as in the creative garage chapel we'd glimpsed on passing, the presence of a deep religious conviction was evident. This was soon reinforced in the next, very large sub-terra hall we entered, more a basilica than simple hall.

This final room was equally amazing. Here Antonio had created a church (*Chiesa de San Antonio?*) in the midst of his wine casks. One entire side of this room was a massive brick wall dotted with niches, each piled high with bottles resting on their sides. In prime position from on high, overlooking this oenological expanse, was a painting of a bishop in full regalia— crook, miter and all. But what kind of church could this be if it lacked an altar? Not to worry, Antonio had thought of everything. This last surprise was the wine grotto altar to outshine all wine grotto altars.

The altar itself was a simple affair, appropriately made from materials on hand—two large barrique oak barrels capped with, I suspect, planks and covered with an oilcloth. Smaller demijohns filled with corks substituted for candles on either side. This rather humble affair, however, was dominated by a giant cross inset in the wall above an irregular stone mantle. Just like the adjacent niche-filled grand wall, it was also decorated with wine bottles lying on their sides. The massive cross took up much of the wall behind the altar. On either side of this main cross was an added lesser cross, each made of bricks in relief so as to be noticeable but not encroach on the effect of the dominate bottle cross.

Having witnessed this cocktail of sights and sampled the *Taurasi*, we soon made our goodbyes to Antonio and rejoined a repentant Margaret to continue our journey. It had been an extraordinary, eye-opening experience ladled out a turn at a time as we moved through Antonio's underworld.

The surprises we experience in life, by their nature, are never planned but add much texture to the breaths we take. Each surprise eclipses the mundane and for the brief instant of its existence, we feel the sudden wonder of the unexpected. How true of the surprises on our trip home to Calitri, thanks to architect, photographer, visionary, and vintner Antonio Caggiano. His world is full of wondrous surprises and more than enough bottles of Taurasi to sip away a lifetime as we try to understand what it all means. Life is an unpaved road full of surprises. Just maybe Margaret was trying to teach us something. In many ways, what matters is who we meet along our way to help navigate life to a happy ending. *Carpe Vinum* (Seize the wine)!

December, 2008

Epilogue

There you have it. A little over two years of tales chronicling the beginning of years of adventures in Italy and especially the discovery of our home away from home, Calitri. To this day, Calitri remains a real place. It continues to live unscathed by mass tourism, outside the typical guidebook's attempt to describe the wonderment that we now know as Italy.

Still not convinced? Still hesitant? Still not sure you should buy a ticket and head off to Italy, or God forbid, take that leap of faith? Then stay tuned for these beginning ramblings of an American couple's first forays into the not-so-familiar environs of Italia are just that, a beginning, and are **To be Continued.**

Look for *Volume II: Living the Dream* to appear soon. It continues our saga from where we left off, on through the years 2009-2010.

67. Pansies on an Italian wall

Photo Index

1. Paolo and Maria Elena relaxing, Lake Como

We are just a few short steps from the lake, sitting at an outdoor cafe in Lenno taking a break after returning from a visit to nearby *Villa del Balbianello* (Ch 17). A glass of wine for Maria Elena, a Peroni beer for me, and the sports newspaper to check on how Team Napoli had fared, was all that was needed.

2. Paolo tries on an ape for size

Here I am in Calitri's *Piazza della Repubblica* by the entrance to the *Borgo* just outside City Hall, called the *Comune*. Close by is Mario's Cafe (Ch 12). I am trying to fit myself into a little three-wheeled motorized utility "trucklet" called an *Ape* (Ah-pay). It is narrow enough to make it through the confines of the *Borgo's* streets. I, however, remain just a bit out of bounds for its miniature cab. Maybe they come with a sun roof?

3. Hillside of the Antico Borgo, Calitri

Here is a view of the medieval labyrinth of historic houses, ours included, called the *Borgo*. Over the centuries this maze of streets has built-up on and into the hillside of Calitri. At the top is the Gesualdo family castle and beyond it, over the ridge, modern Calitri itself. The photo is from adjacent Monte Calvario, home to *Chiesa del Calvario* (Calvery Church) built by a member of the family Gervasi following his return from a crusade to the Holy Land.

4. Face of man on the Street, Taormina Sicily

I had many, many pictures of Italian faces to choose from. I chose this one as it brings back the memory of our visit to Sicily, Taormina to be exact. He looks so innocent. We found him in the town of Fonza D'Agro, just down the street from the Church of *Maria Santa Annunzi* where the wedding scene from the Godfather was filmed. It is said that, to this day, Mafia bosses have their daughters married there. Very respectful toward everyone we met there, I wasn't about to question their judgment.

5. Face of market-day vendor, Calitri

Every Thursday that I've attended the weekly street market, I have seen this woman selling vegetables from the back of her paneled truck. Asked for her photo, she consented with this slightly more than Mona Lisa smile.

6. As we found it in '06, Casa della Feritoia, Calitri

On our tour of possible properties to purchase back in 2006, this is exactly how we found the place we eventually purchased, *Casa della Feritoia*. Weeds, cobwebs, and grass growing on the roof greeted us. Yes, it needed work but we'd seen far worse.

7. Casa della Feritoia in '07, Calitri

About a year later, things had improved inside and, as you can see here, outside as well. I haven't much to do outside. No lawn to clip, only weeds to pull, especially upon our arrival.

8. Front door, Casa della Feritoia today, Calitri Borgo

By now, things have greatly improved. Similar to the previous photo, here is a different perspective of what we then referred to as *Piazza Monico*. We were alone in our little front-door courtyard, the only entry through that arched tunnel. We would sometimes have lunch out there, evidenced by the table. Occasionally a tourist, even more the tourist than us, would come by. The tiles on the wall by the main door are of places in Italy we had visited up to then.

9. Watching fireworks during the passeggiata, Calitri

The men here are watching the fireworks display that surprised us during one *passeggiata*. They are outside of Baby Boom, a baby item shop. The man with his hand raised is our dear friend Francesco, whose daughter, Pasqualina, runs this store.

10. Fireworks, downtown Calitri

One of the evening's fireworks blasts high over our heads, caught after an earlier boom caused us to jump in surprise. We were unaware that this was about to happen, and at first thought the detonation some sort of nasty explosion, which it was, but in a celebratory way.

11. The Tre Rose Osteria tiled sign, Calitri

These tiles adorn the wall announcing you have entered the dining room of the *Tre Rose*, a popular osteria in town. Our host, Michale, along with Mimo (short for Domenic), the waiter, are a delight. While rolled beef *braciole* is not on the menu, it is always available simmering slowly in a pot of sauce back in the kitchen. Just ask Mimo for some!

12. The Saturday night help yourself buffet at Tre Rose, Calitri

This is the help-yourself cold buffet only available on Saturday nights at *Tre Rose*. Let me caution you, the wine is not included. It sits under the TV in a corner of the dining room and although its bounty will vary, for the most part it features pleasing bites of seafood.

13. Tre Rose camaraderie, Calitri

An evening at Tre Rose can be filled with the unexpected. A local hotspot for many townspeople, it is not uncommon to move over a table or two to join with them in conversation and vino. Know them or not, they are as curious about you as you are about them. This photo shows that we've done just that. We learned that this man was a heart surgeon. He along with his friends enjoyed meals at the Tre Rose often. It was about at this point that he was explaining the positive benefits of vino, especially when it came to men. Maria Elena couldn't get over his antics, nor mine. By night's end, what with the food, vine, and the affable good nature of newly made friends, I was so glad we'd decided to spend a night at Tre Rose.

14. Lucia - born, raised, lived, loved, and died in Calitri

This is Lucia who, unfortunately, we only had the pleasure of meeting one time as we wondered through the *Borgo*. She lived a few streets below us. She opened herself and her home to us that day. I miss her.

15. Vito and Maria, Calitri Borgo

Although Vito looks stern here, he was a kind and gentle man. I guess he was not too comfortable having his picture taken. As I wrote, he brought back memories from my TV days watching *The Life of Riley* and reminded me of its star, William Bendix. His wife, Maria, here in her workaday smock, keeper of a fine street garden of the terracotta pot variety, is the epitome of an Italian mom who honestly believes everyone must be hungry and needs to be fed with each visit. I'm so glad she invited us into their lives.

16. Two Marias chat about a potted garden, Calitri Borgo

We met Maria in the street just outside her door one day. We were surprised to find a garden in our concrete neighborhood, since seeing soil is actually a rarity. Her pots arrayed on one side of the street supplied her with not only flowers but everyday staples like tomatoes and basil.

17. Maria serves up an afternoon snack in her kitchen, Calitri Borgo

Not only did we get to enjoy some of Vito's wine but also sampled their homemade salami, which Maria is serving-up here in her kitchen.

18. Sign over the door of the Cinderella Cat, Calitri Borgo

This is the shingle for the Cinderella Cat, just above the entry door. About three streets below us on the mountainside, it is known for its excellent regional cuisine. Most times you'll need a reservation.

19. Author picking grapes, Calitri countryside

Perfect courtroom quality evidence of the point I have made—the grapes on these Italian vines grow much too low to the ground. They seem to have their way with their Italian owners, to the detriment of tall people like myself, my obstinate back having its way with me.

20. Maria Elena harvesting grapes, Calitri countryside

My outdoorsy girl in the vineyard doing her part for the *vendemmia* (wine harvest). Kiss her, she's Irish and my official wine taster.

21. The Statue of the Immigrant, Calitri

This has to be Fulvio's signature piece, his equivalent to *The David.* Not chiseled in marble, his masterpiece is cast and serves in daily testament to all those who, early in the 20th century, departed Calitri seeking a better life.

22. Tommaso at the counter of his shop, Calitri Borgo

My storeowner friend, Tommaso, is a man of many talents. It is common to come by his shop and find him tinkering with some electronic gadget, more than likely to offset hours of tedium. A solar-powered thingamagig or zany invention from the realm of his mind will oftentimes greet you at the door.

23. Fulvio in his art gallery, Calitri Borgo

The Maestro at work in his studio on a bright and sunny day. It is humbling to explore the genius of his gallery, just off of his *laboratorio.* The breadth of his skills and the range of materials he employs is a welcomed blessing to Calitri and anyone who may visit his studio.

24. Lady in the Lily Pond, Calitri Borgo

One of Fulvio's especially interesting works. I called her the *Lady of the Lake*. This juxtaposition of meaning is now gone from his studio, undoubtedly drifted off to some collector's wall.

25. Barista Mario at his station in Mario's Cafe, Calitri

The coffee wizard, smiley Mario himself, as you will find him each morning beside his hissing brewing machine. Open at 7:00 a.m. sharp, cloaked in vest and apron, this purveyor of espresso and wisdom is ready for his many clients, including me. Be sure to chat with him about postcards and aircraft, two of his favorite topics.

26. Caciocavallo cheese curing in the cheese grotto, Calitri Borgo

Each of these globes of cheese dangle in pairs as they cure with a bluish coating of mold inside a humid hollowed-out grotto in the hillside of the Calitri. They owe part of their name, *cavallo*, to the fact that they are reminiscent of saddlebags across the back of a horse or mule. Whatever they choose to call it, this sharp tasting and creamy cheese has been a hit in these parts for centuries.

27. A view deeper into the Borgo underworld, Calitri Borgo

This glass plate was difficult for me to step on, considering that if I were to fall through, it would be goodbye. On closer inspection, it was thick enough to support an elephant. I still gave it a wide berth.

28. Prosciutto grotto kitchen stove, Calitri Borgo

This is a traditional *fornacella* stove used in Calitri to both cook and heat. Below each of the three copper pots, a wood fire can be lit. The square door panels permit access to their individual fire-boxes. The opening by the floor allows a fire to burn and its smoke to exit, with some heat radiating into the kitchen. They could have greatly benefited from a good old Ben Franklin stove back then.

29. Our ragtag team celebrates a successful harvest, Calitri countryside

It was our first experience at harvesting the plump purple beauties. Worn out and tired at this point, we relax by the side of the road after our morning of grape picking. I still recall the mud, which claimed my shoes. To this day they reside in Calitri, ready for the next harvest.

30. Just arrived, Maria Elena waits by our door, Calitri Borgo

Maria Elena got ahead of me somehow. She sits by our door waiting for me, the guy with the keys. She has some of the groceries we picked-up on our drive to Calitri from the airport. There would be many trips back and forth to unload our rental, parked in the piazza. The help of friends was greatly appreciated, since in these early days, we hadn't yet learned to pack lightly and accumulate fewer goodies along the way, enough to fill a car.

31. Joséphine's Market sign, Calitri

When we first came to Calitri, we never realized that there was a local market so close to our home. It was hidden behind a hanging beaded curtain. Until the advent of Josie's sign, or if you were lucky enough to be passing by when Michele, her husband, was unloading boxes of groceries to stock the shelves, you were hard-pressed to realize this gem ever existed. Spanish, English, French, and of course, Italian are spoken here among the aisles of pasta.

32. Carabinieri patrolling Calitri

The local military style police make rounds of the town from time to time. Here they stop to chat in *Piazza della*

Repubblica as I sit one morning, taking in the affairs of the day, in one of Mario's perfectly situated plastic lawn-chairs.

33. Market day olive selection, Calitri

Each Thursday morning is market day in Calitri. Vans with pop-out sides arrive and set up shop marketing everything from clothing to food and everything in between, including CDs and tools. I can't come home without a bag of my favorite olives, enough to get us through the week. Here are tubs of my favorites. I especially like the plump green variety, but thanks to my favorite olive man, I'm always offered a sample of any I'd like in an attempt to add to my buying habits.

34. Oven-ready melanzana-ricotta dish, Casa della Feritoia, Calitri

Maria Elena served this concoction for lunch following our return from the market. You can't get fresher than this, since most likely the eggplant was picked that very day and I know the ricotta from the DiCecca farm outside of town had just been delivered. This gradually became the big meal of our day and, what with wine, no wonder we settled into the habit of taking naps in the afternoon.

35. Maria Elena with the town square boys, Sant'Agata dei Goti

On a once upon a time road trip, we visited Sant'Agata, not far from Benevento. As you can see, my Maria was a hit with the fellas in the town square. We hadn't had any wine yet and there she was in some guy's lap! I'm glad she is game for the fun. Oh, the excitement of being out and about in Italy.

36. Enjoying lunch in Certaldo

Certaldo is a fairytale kind of place. Though small, its charm is magnetic and we have since returned to this Tuscan hilltop town accessible by funicular from its modern counterpart below. Here, we enjoy panini sandwiches along with marinated artichoke hearts. I'd return in a heartbeat.

37. Villa Balbianello, Lake Como

No trip to Lake Como is complete without a visit to this historic villa. Its beautiful gardens and manicured grounds are a mixture of fairytale enchantment and "I want to believe in magic" fantasy. It's no wonder Hollywood has come knocking here more than once.

38. Santa Caterina Hermitage, Lake Maggiore

It is worth the trip across the lake to the small wharf below the cliff wall, home to the Santa Caterina Hermitage. It is a wonder that anyone could have survived on its rock face, let alone create a thriving monastery. It is a true testament to both God's grace and man's devotion.

39. Piazza in Orta San Giulio, Lake Orta

We had lunch on the lawn of a small park by the water's edge off to the side of this square. A small island of picturesque buildings and smaller yet boats out on this Alpine lake added to the quiet beauty of the moment under the shade of a tree.

40. Paolo pays his parking fine, Borgonmanero

Here the on again, off again indecisive author finally chose to fess-up and pay his parking fine before chancing to be pounced on by the *Carabinieri* or something worse. The back of my mind told me Lady Luck might have her way with me if I didn't take care of it then. At the least, I'd have felt guilty and subliminally monitored my rear-view mirror constantly. How refreshing a clear conscience can be.

41. Maria Elena on commuter train, Rome

And to think, she thought she could laugh while I kept the train police at bay. Little did she realize at the time that she too was in violation of the 24-hour ticket rule and the fine would have been double!

42. The Doge Palace, Venice

Maria Elena's favorite city in all of *Italia*, Venice, is depicted here by its iconic skyline, the Doge Palace in St Mark's Square. A little of the very rogue Casanova himself must have worn off on me following my visit to the Doge Palace and its secret venue—subject to disclosure in a yet to come story in a future volume.

43. Our suitcase burdened group in Venice

We somehow managed to arrive in Venice even though we lacked beasts of burden capable of carrying all of our luggage. Instead, we were the pack animals. Praise to the person who thought of wheels on suitcases! It was a small miracle they let us on the *vaporetto* water buses with all this luggage. Along with my sister and brother-in-law, we hesitated here to get our bearings. Little did we realize that our accommodations were right behind us, down the narrow alley, just barely visible.

44. Our agro-tourism cottage in Chiusi, Tuscany

This was our guest cottage, surrounded by olive groves and oak forests, at Poggio Pilella in Chiusi. It was a welcomed opportunity to depressurize and relax from the pace of Venice and Florence before continuing on to Calitri.

45. Typical Carabinieri patrol car, Lucca

A mainstream, *Smokey and the Bandit*, hot-pursuit police vehicle regularly seen throughout Italy. They keep a close watch on everything. At random traffic stops, the police use massive ledgers, resting atop their vehicle hoods, to log the details of each driver they've pulled over flashing their oversized ping-pong paddles. In Alaska, I recall watching bears snag salmon from the riverbanks. Like them, these "bears" are not to be messed with as they snag their prey. The thing usually swung over their necks, like a purse, is a machine gun, which explains why I quickly lose my roguish manner and assume an obedient lap-dog nature whenever I'm stopped.

46. Friendly pair of police officers, Florence

I tried to trade hats with these two but only got this smile in the deal. Surprisingly, they let me take their picture. They are not *Carabinieri* but instead are some sort of city police. The parachute wings on one of their uniforms, however, does suggest a military nature to their trade.

47. The Temple of Ceres, Paestum

Why go to Greece when Greece can come to you in nearby Paestum? Though earthquakes come and go here, this 2,500 year old temple still stands, along with its two neighboring temples. Dedicated to Ceres, the Roman goddess of agriculture, fertility and motherly relationships, it is the smallest of the three Paestum temples. The discovery of three Christian tombs in its floor indicate that at some point it was also used as a Christian house of worship. Interestingly, while Christians held services inside, Greek tradition reserved the temple as the home of the god or goddess, with rituals held outside.

48. Dandelion on Cardo Maximus, Paestum

I hope you can make it out, because this single, simple, yellow flower captured my attention the day we visited the long-dead city of Paestum. It was the only color in an otherwise gray field of proud stones that once came together to form this once great metropolis. In defiance, its bristly head thrust itself up toward the sky through stone ruts carved into the road's surface by the incessant turning of chariot wheels. I'd discovered life in Paestum.

49. Grillo D'Oro restaurant, Bisaccia

Looking more like an apartment building, this rather modern looking structure, on the outskirts of Bisaccia, is home to The Golden Cricket. I like the drive over from Calitri along a road winding through phalanxes of churning wind turbines. I sometimes wonder about the origin of its name. I just never remember to ask, for once inside, I adore listening to what is being offered that evening. With no printed menu, it's a grab-bag of anticipation as you await what the waiter brings to your table. We have never been disappointed.

50. Roadside wind turbines, Bisaccia

Not a drawing, these are the real thing. They are enormous and provide Calitri with the majority of its electrical needs.

51. Grillo D'Oro ceiling poem to the winds, Bisaccia

Along the ceiling partitions in *Grillo D'Oro* you will find poetic expressions. This is just one of them. With all the turbines in the area, you are correct to surmise that it's a windy area. That's what is being expressed here ... you are in the midst of the wind, a wind even when you are still.

52. Maria Elena and Geraldina enjoying themselves at Grillo D'Oro, Bisaccia

Maria Elena and friend Gerardina yukking it up after dinner. I don't recall what triggered their laughter, but then it doesn't take much.

53. The wild boar hunter, Bisaccia

Looking very much like he'd done this many times before, I discovered him there by the side of the road waiting to be picked up to go hunting for the elusive wild boar (*cinghiale*) lurking in the nearby forests.

54. Author, Antonio, Maria Elena, and Carl, Montella

It was cool at the festival in Montella that night. My hands must have gotten cold, because soon after this picture was snapped, I dropped the camera in my hand and ruined the lens. Ouch. But at that moment we were all smiles, especially Carl there on the right with his gleaming, white, new teeth courtesy of Costa Rica.

55. Chestnut warehouse, Montella

Chestnuts are big business in Montella. They are so good that they have earned an official seal of approval similar to Italian wines with their DOC and even more prestigious DOCG designations. Chestnuts earn an IGP (*Indicazione Geografica Tipica*) protective mark of authenticity though any reasonable person might think it should be IGT! This commercial warehouse was stocked full.

56. Roasted wild boar with sunglasses, Montella

I'd seen pigs with apples in their mouths before but never one wearing sunglasses, whether alive or slow-turned roasted. While the absurdity of it gets your attention, its juicy flavor in a sandwich will quickly soothe any appetite.

57. Scraping melted caciocavallo cheese, Montella

Caciocavallo cheese, dangling inches above the scarlet coals of an evening fire, softens to a buttery consistency before being generously smeared over inch thick fire-toasted bread. This simple yet delicious snack hits the spot during the cool autumn evenings of the Montella chestnut festival.

58. The Lancelot Hotel's common patio area, Rome

We made good use of this Hotel Lancelot terrace during our stay in Rome. By night, visible through the greenery to the left, rose the floodlight lit walls of the Coliseum. A little cheese, salami and much vino, and you would swear you could hear the roar of ancient crowds.

59. Close-up of the lantern atop St. Peter's, Rome

I cropped and zoomed this photo enough to focus on what is called the Lantern. If you are lucky enough to survive the trek, you'll exit onto a circular terrace at the base of the Lantern that affords views of the Vatican grounds and greater Rome that relatively few get to see. I have no idea of what those who don't make it receive, but I suspect as a minimum, an EKG and nitro-glycerin tablet would be in order.

60. Maria Elena ascending the Vatican dome staircase, Rome

This is a look back at Maria Elena as she ascends what could be called the stairway to heaven. It is situated between the inner and outer shells of St. Peter's dome. By this time, the smile has left her face at the realization that we had willingly paid for this torturous assent.

61. View from the lantern, Rome

Looking just about due east, this is the bird's-eye view that greeted us across St. Peter's Square and beyond, across greater Rome. To our left (not visible in this scene) were the gardens outside of the Vatican Museum and the roof atop the Sistine Chapel. In truth, it was worth all the huffing and puffing to reach this spectacular vantage point.

62. View from St. Peter's square toward where we'd been, Rome

Standing just about on the border between Italy and the Vatican, we took one last look back at where we had been. High and mighty no longer, we once again resumed our mortal roles upon the Earth.

63. Waiting for a wine delivery, Taurasi

As the town slept in the heat of afternoon, Maria Elena relaxes on the steps of a local Taurasi bar. As we waited for our newfound wine entrepreneur to return, little did we realize what awaited us beneath our feet—a subterranean world dedicated to the only DOCG designated wine in all of southern Italy, the sun's very own nectar, Taurasi!

64. Cantine Antonio Caggiano, Taurasi

Our visit to this *cantina* unexpectedly led to the exploration of what lay beneath the roots of the Taurasi vineyards. Signor Caggiano himself gave us the grand tour of the world he has created below ground. Himself an accomplished photographer, Antonio taught me between drags on a cigar, a cigar never extending beyond the length of his nose, how to best use one of my camera settings. I'd take further classes there any day.

65. Cantine Antonio Caggiano wine storage grotto, Taurasi

In addition to rooms filled with oak wine barrels, there were many hollowed-out grottos like this one. Each was stocked full with hundreds of bottles of Taurasi wine of various vintages. I'm told that well stored bottles can sell for up to $400 each! Though far far more modestly priced, the bottles we purchased went down just fine. I fear that if I ever had a goblet of the really pricy stuff, I doubt I'd ever get to taste it. My hand, shaking so much from nervousness over the pricy nectar, would insure the goblet would be empty by the time it reached my lips.

66. Cantine Antonio Caggiano little people figurines, Taurasi

At one point, we rounded a bend and emerged into a miniature world of carved figurines. This particular one is a caricature of Antonio Caggiano himself waving goodbye to us in fitting salute to this, the ending to Volume I, Discovering Calitri.

67. Pansies on an Italian wall

My neo-realistic impressions of Italy see it today in flux between its historic past and a demanding, though unknowable, future. Life today can be symbolized by these flowers, while life as it once was is captured in the wall mounted ring, formerly used to tether some medieval horse. Resilient as they have proven to be in the ebbs and tides of time, I'll side with the Italian family to stay the course and keep watering the flowers. All the more reason to return to see how their story continues to unfold.

Coming Soon...

The Italian Chronicles of a Rogue Tourist

Volume II
Living the Dream

The author can be reached for comments at

roguetourist@gmail.com